Applause for Pete Hamill's

WHY SINATRA MATTERS

"A snazzy ode to 'Ole Blue Eyes.'" — *People*

"Compelling reading for anyone with a feeling for the late singer."
— Adam Woog, *Seattle Times*

"An engrossing book . . . sharply evocative."
— Don Freeman, *San Diego Union-Tribune*

"Hamill conveys moments with memories so vivid that you can
smell the smoke and taste the bourbon."
— Vicki L. Friedman, *Virginian-Pilot*

"This is a beautiful thing, an admiring rumination on Sinatra the
man, the persona, and the towering talent. . . . An absolutely terrific
work." — Liz Smith, *Newsday*

"Hamill's illuminations are considerable. . . . Any Sinatra fan hungry
for a fresh take will eat up *Why Sinatra Matters.*"
— Dan DeLuca, *Philadelphia Inquirer*

"Even if you think you know why Sinatra matters, this slim bio-
graphical essay proves the most intimate and thoughtful eulogy for
'the Voice' yet. . . . Hamill's concise, eloquent musings leave you
wanting not to read a full-blown biography but to listen again to
Sinatra's best songs." — Megan Harlan, *Entertainment Weekly*

"What a perfect match: the world's greatest 'saloon singer' eulogized
superbly by the author of *A Drinking Life*. . . . *Why Sinatra Matters*
belongs in any collection of important books on American popular
music of the 20th century." — *Kirkus Reviews*

"The only thing wrong with this brief but penetrating essay is that it
is far too short." — Terry Teachout, *New York Times Book Review*

WHY SINATRA
MATTERS

. . .

PETE
HAMILL

LITTLE, BROWN AND COMPANY
BOSTON NEW YORK LONDON

Originally published in hardcover by Little, Brown and Company, October 1998
First Back Bay paperback edition, May 2003

Photo Credits: Archive Photos: endpapers, page 90; Dennis Stock/Magnum
Photos Inc.: page ii; Penguin/Corbis Bettmann, page 34; Personality Photos,
page 66; UPI/Corbis Bettmann, page 124; Sid Avery/Motion Picture and Television Photo Archive, page 154

ISBN 0-316-34796-5 (hc) / 0-316-73886-7 (pb)
Library of Congress Control Number 98-67480

10   9   8   7   6   5   4   3   2   1

Q-FF

Book design by Michael Ian Kaye

Printed in the United States of America

THIS BOOK IS FOR
ESTHER NEWBERG
She can make the rain go

WHY SINATRA MATTERS

■ ■ ■

OVERTURE

W HEN F RANK S INATRA died on the evening of May
14, 1998, the news made the front pages of newspapers all
over the world. Many ran extra editions and followed
with special supplements. There was little sense of shock;
he had been a long time dying. He had also been a long
time living, and so the obituaries were full of his life and
times.

It was mandatory to chronicle his wins and losses, his
four marriages, his battles, verbal and physical, with reporters and photographers. His romances required
many inches of type. There were accounts of his fierce
temper, his brutalities, his drunken cruelties. Some described him as a thug or a monster, whose behavior was
redeemed only by his talent. We read brief charts of his

political odyssey from left to right. The shadow cast upon him by the Mob was also an inevitable part of the stories. And there were tales of his personal generosity to friends and strangers and the millions of dollars he had raised for charities. He was clearly a complicated man.

"Being an eighteen-karat manic depressive," he was quoted in many of the obituaries, "and having lived a life of violent emotional contradictions, I have perhaps an overacute capacity for sadness and elation."

But much of the language of farewell had a stale, even hollow quality, probably because most of the obituaries had been ready for too many months. Sinatra had been a virtual recluse since 1995, making only rare public appearances. Over the previous year he had been in and out of hospitals. There were reports from California that he had suffered several heart attacks and, with the possible onset of Alzheimer's, had difficulty recognizing even old friends. Across those final months there was little hard news about his condition; his children insisted he was fine, although cranky and cantankerous, and so the vacuum was filled with rumor and supposition. The truth was probably a simple one. Frank Sinatra, after a life in which too many cigarettes and too much whiskey were part of the deal, was old; and as happens to all of us when we grow old, the parts just broke down. He had abused his body in a way that was special to his generation of American men; that he had survived until eighty-two was itself a kind of triumph over the odds.

There were some peculiar components to the television coverage. Most of it was narrated by people from a much younger generation; as they mouthed words about loss and farewell, the tone had an odd insincerity – they could have been discussing someone from the nineteenth century. They were also prisoners of existing visual images. We saw Sinatra at different ages: a very young Sinatra in bow tie and padded shoulders when he was The Voice; a drawn, emaciated Sinatra, flaring at photographers or wearing a thin, pimplike mustache, during his time with Ava Gardner; Sinatra as Maggio in *From Here to Eternity* and a grinning Sinatra receiving his Academy Award afterward; clips from his television shows, including a bizarre image of Sinatra standing on two chairs, one foot on each, while singing "I've Got the World on a String"; Sinatra with the Rat Pack, horsing around on the stages of Las Vegas; Sinatra with various presidents, from Roosevelt to Reagan; and, of course, endless versions of "My Way."

It was difficult, reading and watching all of this, to remember why Sinatra mattered to so many people, and why he will continue to matter in the years ahead. The radio did a much better job than print or television, because on radio we heard the music. Not abrupt fragments of songs, not clipped, impatient digests. Late at night, driving through a great city, moving on the dark streets of New York or Paris, Tokyo or London, you could connect more directly to what truly mattered: the music.

The music was the engine of the life. If there had been no music, there would have been no immense obituaries and no televised farewells. To be sure, Sinatra was one of those figures whose art is often overshadowed by the life. In the end, it is of minor interest that Lord Byron swam the Hellespont, that André Malraux flew in combat during the Spanish Civil War, or that Ernest Hemingway shot lions in Africa. In the end, only the work matters. Sinatra's finest work was making music.

Sinatra, however, did matter in other ways. He wasn't simply an entertainer from a specific time and place in American life who lived on as a kind of musty artifact. Through a combination of artistic originality, great passion, and immense will, he transcended several eras and indirectly helped change the way all of us lived. He was formed by an America that is long gone: the country of the European immigrants and the virulent America-for-Americans nativism that was directed at them; the country in which a mindless Puritanism, allied with that scapegoating nativism, imposed Prohibition upon the land and helped create the Mob; a country undergoing a vast transformation from a fundamentally rural society to one dominated by cities; a country that passed through Depression and war into the uncertain realities of peace. They were extraordinary times, and in his own way, driven by his own confusions, neuroses, angers, and ambitions, Frank Sinatra helped push the country forward.

This book is about the accomplishments of Frank Sinatra and why he matters. Some of it is personal, because for a while, I was friendly with Sinatra, talked with him in saloons, in Las Vegas, even for a few days one year in Monte Carlo. At one point he wanted me to write his autobiography; it never happened, for reasons that are no longer important. But in the course of discussing his life, he talked about himself in ways that still had an element of wonder to them; part of him still could not believe that he had become the legend he was. To be sure, we were not friends in any conventional way; I did not visit his home and he did not visit mine. Only a very few intimate friends ever had such access, and I was certainly not one of them. But I liked him enormously.

■　■　■

He was wonderful with children, including my two daughters. He was funny. He was vulnerable. I never saw the snarling bully of the legend. That Frank Sinatra certainly existed; on the day that his death made all those front pages, there were too many people who remembered only his cruelties. But he never showed that side of himself when I was around. On those nights, I was in the company of an intelligent man, a reader of books, a lover of painting and classical music and sports, gallant with women, graceful with men. Perhaps he was just donning a mask in my company, presenting images to a writer so that they would be remembered by the writer in a certain way: a kind of performance. Or perhaps the snarling bully was the true masked character, a clumsy personal invention, and behind the mask there was simply a young man afraid of the world. Or perhaps, by the time I knew him, he had just grown out of his angers, exhausted them, and settled for what he was and the way he was regarded. I don't know. Like all great artists, Frank Sinatra contained secret places, abiding personal mysteries, endless contradictions. On occasion, a curtain would part, there would be a moment of epiphany, and I could see the uncertain older man who wanted to understand what it all meant, the man who said that dying was a pain in the ass. I liked that man very much.

This book does not pretend to be the final word on Frank Sinatra. Several full-scale biographies have already been written, each with its attendant excellencies; more are sure to follow. But there were aspects of this man that should be remembered and honored. In Sinatra's time, his fame as a singer spread from his own country to the world. His turbulent personality, often shadowed by notoriety, seemed inseparable from the style and originality of his art and gave him an essential place on the public stage of the American century. Now Sinatra is gone, taking with him all his anger, cruelty, generosity, and personal style. The music remains. In times to come, that music will continue to matter, whatever happens to our evolving popular culture. The world of my grandchildren will not listen to Sinatra in the way four generations of Americans have listened to him. But high art always survives. Long after his death, Charlie Parker still plays his version of the urban blues. Billie Holiday still whispers her anguish. Mozart still erupts in joy. Every day, in cities and towns all over the planet, someone discovers them for the first time and finds in their art that mysterious quality that makes the listener more human. In their work all great artists help transcend the solitude of individuals; they relieve the ache of loneliness; they supply a partial response to the urging of writer E. M. Forster: "Only connect." In their ultimate triumph over the banality of death, such artists continue to matter. So will Frank Sinatra.

HE HAD COME A LONG WAY TO THIS
BLUE LAWN AND HIS DREAM MUST HAVE
SEEMED SO CLOSE THAT HE COULD
HARDLY FAIL TO GRASP IT. HE DID NOT
KNOW THAT IT WAS ALREADY BEHIND
HIM, SOMEWHERE BACK IN THAT VAST
OBSCURITY BEYOND THE CITY, WHERE
THE DARK FIELDS OF THE REPUBLIC
ROLLED ON UNDER THE NIGHT.

—F. SCOTT FITZGERALD,
The Great Gatsby

■ ■ ■

I'M FOR WHATEVER
GETS YOU THROUGH
THE NIGHT.

—FRANK SINATRA

· 1 ·

IN THE
WEE SMALL
HOURS

THIS WAS ON A NEW YORK midnight in 1970. A
hard spring rain had emptied Third Avenue, and neon
lights scribbled garishly across the glistening black as-
phalt. From the front window of P. J. Clarke's saloon, you
could see a few taxis cruising slowly among the spokes of
ruined umbrellas and a trash basket lying on its side, its
contents turning to pulp. Across the street, two old rum-
mies huddled in the doorway of an antique store.

On this night in the rain-drowned city, we were safe
and dry at an oak table in the back room of the saloon.
Clarke's was, and remains, a place out of another time,
all burnished wood and chased mirrors, Irish flags and
browning photographs of prizefighters. A few aging men
at the long, bright bar could gaze out the windows and

still see the Third Avenue El, gone since 1955, or the Irish tenements that were smashed into rubble and replaced with steel-and-glass office buildings. They were each drinking alone and looked as if they remembered other nights too, evoked by the music of the jukebox.

> *What good is the scheming,*
> *the planning and dreaming,*
> *That comes with each*
> *new love affair . . .*

The man singing for the lonesome men at the bar was at our table. Or more precisely, we were at his table. Anytime Frank Sinatra sat down at a table, it became his table. On this night he was in New York for a concert and he was in good spirits. To begin with, the hands of the clock had passed twelve, and he was in a large city, specifically the hard, wounded metropolis of New York. For decades now, Sinatra had defined the glamour of the urban night. It was both a time and a place; to inhabit the night, to be one of its restless creatures, was a small act of defiance, a shared declaration of freedom, a refusal to play by all those conventional rules that insisted on men and women rising at seven in the morning, leaving for work at eight, and falling exhausted into bed at ten o'clock that night. In his music, Sinatra gave voice to all those who believed that the most intense living begins at midnight: show people, bartenders, and sporting women; gamblers, detectives, and gangsters; small winners and big losers; artists and newspapermen. If you loved someone who did not love you back, you could always walk into a saloon, put your money on the bar, and listen to Sinatra.

Here in one of the late-night places of an all-night city, Sinatra was wearing a dark suit, a perfectly knotted red tie, a pale blue shirt, silver cuff links, and was drinking Jack Daniel's. He was still lean then. The famous face remained an arrangement of knobs and planes that didn't assemble into any conventional version of masculine handsomeness but had an enormous vitality; it was a face that defeated painters and seduced photographers. His eyes were bright and blue (although nobody had yet called him Old Blue Eyes), and the mouth was mobile and expressive. He had a wonderful smile. The voice, of course, was a whiskey-and-cigarettes baritone.

He sat with his back against the wall in the muted light of the room and seemed to ignore his own voice on the jukebox. He was facing Danny Lavezzo, who ran Clarke's; William B. Williams, the disc jockey who had christened Sinatra "the Chairman of the Board"; Jilly Rizzo, who ran a saloon across town and had been one of Sinatra's best friends for more than twenty years; two young women whose faces were too perfect; and the sportswriter Jimmy Cannon. The table was crowded with glasses, ashtrays, bowls of peanuts and pretzels. Only Cannon sipped coffee. There were about eight other people at smaller tables, and you could see the rain racing down one of the small side windows. Lavezzo made certain the other customers were kept at a distance by seating them as far from Sinatra's table as possible without handing them umbrellas. The sound of "When Your Lover Has Gone" made Cannon turn his head toward the jukebox.

"That's the saddest goddamned song ever written," he said.

"It's right up there," Sinatra said, shaking his head and lighting an unfiltered Camel with a heavy silver lighter.

"You know where it's from?" Cannon said. "It's from a terrible movie called *Blonde Crazy.* Cagney and Joanie. 1931."

"Joanie who?" said Jilly Rizzo, his bad eye gleaming. "Crawford?"

"Blondell, dummy," Sinatra said. "Joan Blondell. Cannon used to go with her."

"You're kidding me," Rizzo said. "You went with Joan Blondell? A busted-down *sportswriter* went out with Joan Blondell?"

"He didn't always look this bad," Sinatra said. Cannon smiled in an embarrassed way. He was a small man with a long, pudgy Irish face and horn-rimmed glasses.

"It was a long time ago," Cannon said. He looked relieved when the song ended, but its lonesome mood seemed to stain the air around him.

Rizzo turned to one of the young women. "You ever hear of Joan Blondell?"

The young woman shrugged. No.

"What about Cagney? You know, *James Cagney?*"

"I know him," said the second woman brightly. "He was the guy, the captain, in that picture with Henry Fonda, right? About the navy?"

"You win a dish of strawberries, sweetheart," Sinatra said.

"I don't like strawberries," she said in a baffled way. Sinatra laughed out loud. So did the rest of us, but it wasn't until I was home, hours later, that I realized Sinatra had mixed up the strawberries scene from *The Caine Mutiny* with the potted palm scene from *Mister Roberts.* We'd all laughed with him, but the young woman was right to be baffled.

After a while Rizzo got up to take the two young women to a taxi while the conversation roamed in other directions. Somehow it arrived at writers. Was Ernest Hemingway greater than F. Scott Fitzgerald? Cannon insisted on the superiority of Hemingway. Sinatra preferred Fitzgerald.

"That *Great Gatsby,* come on, Jimmy, Hemingway couldn't do that."

"Yeah, but he could do a lot of other things," Cannon said. "And Fitzgerald could only do that one thing."

Rizzo returned and sat down. Cannon turned to me, the only other writer at the table: "What do you think?"

I repeated something Dizzy Gillespie once told me in an interview: "The professional is the guy that can do it twice."

"Wow, is *that* true," Sinatra said. "About *everything*. That's a great line."

"Yeah, and it's a vote for Hemingway," Cannon said. On the jukebox, Sinatra was singing "You Make Me Feel So Young."

"What about you, Jilly? Hemingway or Fitzgerald?"

"Hey, no contest," Jilly said, deadpan. "Ella all the way."

They all laughed, and then the talk shifted, and "Don't Worry 'Bout Me" was on the juke, and the waiter brought another round and clean ashtrays. Someone wanted to know the name of the worst living American. The nominations flowed and ebbed: Walter O'Malley, Mitch Miller, Richard Nixon ("Come on, lay off," said Sinatra, who had supported Nixon over George McGovern). But then another name was offered and in a rush of enthusiasm, the table unanimously voted the title of worst living American to the boxer Jake La Motta.

"He dumped the fight to Billy Fox, and *never told his father,* who bet his life savings on Jake," Sinatra said. "Lower than whale shit."

And from La Motta, they moved seamlessly to Sugar Ray Robinson, another creature of the New York night. During the Depression Robinson had come down from Harlem to dance for pennies in the doorways of Times

Square. Then he had become a fighter of extraordinary grace and power. He had owned a couple of apartment houses in Harlem, a lavender Cadillac, a bar called Sugar Ray's, where women arrived each night to find him, and then lost them all. An accountant took all of Robinson's money to the racetrack, and the fighter had to go back to a sport he no longer loved. Still, he had fought La Motta six times, winning five, including a thirteenth-round knockout that gave him the middleweight championship in a brutal fight in Chicago in 1951. In the fighter's great days, Cannon and Robinson had been close; we didn't know it that night, but Sinatra had privately arranged to support Robinson after the old champion moved to California. They all knew him.

"He used to come in here all the time," Lavezzo said. "He was some beautiful-looking guy." I had seen Robinson's fierce 1957 war with Carmen Basilio, watched him a lot in the old Stillman's Gym, and had covered Robinson's sad last fight, a loss to Joey Archer in 1965 when Sugar Ray was forty-four. Sinatra remembered seeing Robinson knock out Jackie Wilson in Los Angeles in 1947. "You couldn't believe it," he said. "The hand speed, the power, the fucking *elegance*." Jilly saw him decision Kid Gavilan in New York in 1948, and Williams and Lavezzo recalled specific rounds from the two fights with Basilio and the one-punch knockout of Gene Fullmer in the spring of '57. They all talked with a kind of reverence.

"What was it the guy said?" Sinatra said. "There was Ray Robinson, and then there was the top ten."

There was something else floating around in the talk about Robinson. They were all from the same generation, and Robinson symbolized that generation in the same way that Sinatra did. Nobody said so at the table in Clarke's, but they knew it. If Sinatra had not been there (for ass-kissing was not part of the style), someone would have said, There's Sinatra, and then there's the top ten.

Suddenly, Sinatra rose from his seat, excusing himself. A few other patrons looked at him. A woman in her forties widened her eyes and whispered across the table to her man, who turned for a glance. Lavezzo tensed; Clarke's was not the sort of place that encouraged customers to ask for autographs. From the speakers, Sinatra's exuberant voice was now singing "I've Got the World on a String." He was telling the world that he could make the rain go.

"Hey, Danny, don't you have anything on the jukebox besides this dago kid?" Sinatra said to Lavezzo. The saloonkeeper laughed and got up too. Sinatra led the way into a narrow passageway that opened into the front room. A large unsmiling man rose from a small table and followed them. In Clarke's, Sinatra didn't need directions to get to the john.

"He looks good, Jilly," Cannon said.

"Better than ever," Jilly said.

"I wish he'd give up the goddamned Camels," Williams said.

"That's like asking him to give up broads," Jilly said.

"He should give up *marrying* broads," said Cannon, a lifelong bachelor.

There was another voice on the jukebox now. Billie Holiday. She was singing "Mean to Me" in the scraped, hurt voice of her last years. From the Ray Ellis album with strings. *Lady in Satin.*

"This album always makes me want to cry," Williams said.

"Just don't cry into the whiskey," Rizzo said. "Makes it too salty." Cannon smiled. He'd given up whiskey in the 1940s but never gave up the night shift. Whiskey was a big part of nights in that city, and he knew it was futile to deliver sermons to his friends.

"What makes *you* cry, Jilly?" Cannon asked.

"Poverty," Jilly answered. And he laughed out loud.

Then Sinatra was coming back through the passage-way, with the large dour man guarding his back. Two young women stared from the far end of the passage, giggling and tentative, as if having a small debate, and then turned back.

"You know what I love most about this joint?" Sina-tra said. "Taking a piss. Those urinals ... You could stand Abe Beame in one of them and have room to spare."

"The really great thing is the ice at the bottom," Cannon said. "It's like drilling a tunnel."

"That's *power*," Sinatra said, laughing, reaching for the Camels. Lavezzo returned, looking as if he'd just flown a combat mission.

"That better?" he said, gesturing toward the unseen speakers and the anguished voice of Lady Day.

"Like fine wine," Sinatra said, allowing smoke to leak from his mouth. I glanced at my watch. 2:25, the rain still falling. Cannon sipped his coffee. Jilly smothered a yawn. Then Billie Holiday began to sing "I'm a Fool to Want You." A song out of Sinatra's past. Out of 1951 and Ava Gardner and the most terrible time of his life. Everybody at the table knew the story. Sinatra stared for a beat at the bourbon in his glass. Then shook his head.

"Time to go," he said.

We all rose and went to the side door and followed Frank Sinatra into the night.

II. That night came back to me, along with a dozen others, when I heard that Frank Sinatra was dead at eighty-two. I was in the Miami airport, catching an early flight back to New York, after sitting on a panel about the future of newspapers. I had checked in and picked up my boarding pass. Then I saw about a dozen people staring up at a monitor. CNN. The announcer looking grave. I couldn't hear the sound. But then there were some clips and the legend "Frank Sinatra 1915–1998." And I was like all the others in that sterile morning place, sliding into the blurred places of memory.

There was a radio on the window ledge in the kitchen of the tenement in Brooklyn. Through that window, past the radio, out across the backyards, we could see the skyline of New York to the right and the Statue of Liberty in the harbor and the low ridge of Staten Island and the gray smudge of New Jersey beyond. The harbor was thick with ships, heading off through the Narrows to the war. Sometimes the sky was dark with B-17s. At night the skyline vanished into blackness, the lights turned off, as were so many other things, for the duration. There was no television then, and so the radio served us kids as narration and sound track. From that little Philco, we heard about the invasion of North Africa and the assault on Sicily and the fighting at Anzio. The story of the war was all mixed up with the crooning of Bing Crosby and the score from *Oklahoma!* and the Andrews Sisters and Glenn Miller and, at some point, Frank Sinatra.

All or nothing at all . . .

On days of snow or rain, when we could not go down the three flights to the street, those words drifted through the railroad flat. They seemed thin, even trembling, unlike the confident baritone of Crosby, but there was a kind of defiance in them too. I was six when the war started in 1941, and my brother Tommy was two years younger; we were too innocent to connect Sinatra's words to a longing for women. They seemed to be about unconditional surrender, as declared by Franklin D. Roosevelt, whose picture was up on the kitchen wall. It was as if Sinatra were saying the words to Hitler and Tojo. We're coming to get you. And it's all or nothing at all.

In the neighborhood we began to hear arguments among the kids just older than us. Crosby versus Sinatra arguments. They had nothing to do with the words. And it was not simply another division between the Italian American kids and the Irish American kids. Some of the Irish guys were Sinatra fans; some of the Italians went for Crosby. It was about his sound. And sometimes about other things.

There were always newspapers in our flat. The *News* and the *Mirror*, the *Journal-American* and the *Brooklyn Eagle*. And they began printing stories about Sinatra. The Voice. Swoonatra. Hysterical girls roaring at the Paramount, over in Manhattan, which we called New York. In June 1944 the Allies invaded France, heading for Berlin, and the lights went on again in the mighty skyline. For weeks after D-Day I would go up to the roof alone and stare at the skyline, glittering and impossibly beautiful, like the towers of Oz. And from the open windows of the tenements I could hear the battle between Crosby and Sinatra.

I was too young to choose sides. But my father was

definitely a Crosby man. He was a good singer and could deliver pretty fair Crosby renditions at christenings or wakes or from his spot at the bar of Rattigan's. In dinner-table discussion my mother was also a fan of Crosby. But in the Brooklyn mornings she always listened to Martin Block on WNEW, and that meant she also listened to Frank Sinatra. She would sing along with him in her light soprano voice, not judging the music but embracing it. Still, among the immigrants in the neighborhood, Crosby was generally triumphant. He was all over the radio. The few people who owned phonographs played him all the time. (We did not own one.) The jukebox in Rattigan's Bar, across the street, was fat with Crosby 78s, and in the summer you could hear him singing through the open doors. He was sunny. He was optimistic. He was casual. He said we had to accentuate the positive, ee-liminate the negative, and not mess with mister in-between. He said that if we didn't give a feather or a fig, we could grow up to be a pig.

In addition, Crosby had played a priest in *Going My Way*. A *Catholic* priest, for God's sake, whose best friend was an Irishman from Ireland, an older priest played by Barry Fitzgerald. In the movie, which the whole neighborhood went to see during the summer of 1944, Father Crosby saved Father Fitzgerald's run-down parish, St. Dominic's, by writing songs, and the church was in a neighborhood that looked very much like ours. Ordinar-

ily, that would have been enough for my father, who was
an immigrant from Ireland, as was my mother. But there
was still another factor.

Our small part of America was seeing many things
through the prism of the war. We lived in a working-class
neighborhood of Irish, Italian, and Jewish Americans;
most of its young men were off at the war. It was the kind
of neighborhood that provided troops for the infantry,
and in many windows, as the war ground on, there were
small flags bearing gold stars, indicating that one of the
young soldiers would be young forever. My father didn't
go to the war. He had lost his left leg while playing soccer
in the immigrant leagues in 1927; the bones were smashed,
gangrene set in overnight, penicillin did not yet exist,
and they amputated in the morning. Crosby didn't go because he was too old, but in the judgment of the neighborhood, he did the next best thing: he made many trips
for the USO, entertaining troops in the company of co-
medians and beautiful women. But Sinatra was a separate case; he was the right age and he had two arms and
two legs. Why couldn't he do what stars such as Clark
Gable, Glenn Miller, or Jimmy Stewart were doing, and
insist on being taken by one of the armed forces? Why
couldn't he at least make a USO tour?

The male anger against Sinatra came to a head in October 1944, when he played the Paramount again and
30,000 mostly female fans erupted into a small riot outside the theater. When a male dissenter in the Para-

mount balcony fired a tomato at the stage, he had to be rescued from women who were trying to beat him to death. Breathless accounts of these events were all over the newspapers and the radio. At the same time, the first V-2 rockets were falling on London and American troops were fighting their way into Germany, taking heavy casualties. In our neighborhood, where the war was not a distant abstraction, the phenomenon of young Frank Sinatra was discussed with much heat in the bars and on the street corners and in the kitchens.

I don't get it, my father would say. All those girls going nuts for a draft dodger.

He's not a draft dodger, my mother would say. He's 4-F. He's got a punctured eardrum. He tried to join three times, and they turned him down. It was in the papers.

The papers, he sneered. You believe the papers?

Flying north from Florida, I could remember all that argument and my own youthful wonder about its passion. At nine, I was too young to understand what Sinatra was doing with his music. I did know it was different. Crosby made us feel comfortable and, in some larger way, *American.* But there was a tension in Sinatra, an anxiety that we were too young to name but old enough to feel. During the last six months of the European war, when men were dying by the thousands in the Battle of the Bulge, it was confusing to hear songs that contained so much anguish. Or loss. Or loneliness. I would see young women pushing strollers along the avenue, their men off at war, see them pausing to look at the front pages on the newsstands, see the way their faces clenched, and I wished that Bing Crosby could sing to them and make them feel better. It took me a long while to understand that it was Frank Sinatra who was giving words and voice to the emotions of their own roiled hearts.

III. Years later, when I was a reporter and then a columnist for Dorothy Schiff's *New York Post,* I got to know Sinatra. Cannon introduced me to him after the Floyd Patterson–Sonny Liston fight in Las Vegas in 1963. We were together on other evenings. On the surface, this seemed strange, another contradiction in the character of a man dense with contradictions. Sinatra had wasted too much of his adult life in vicious quarrels with newspapermen and gossip columnists, had punched out at least one columnist (the awful Lee Mortimer), and was continually in rumbles with paparazzi.

"Sinatra's idea of paradise is a place where there are plenty of women and no newspapermen," said Humphrey Bogart, who was sixteen years older than the singer and a kind of hero to the younger man. "He doesn't know it, but he'd be better off if it were the other way around."

Perhaps, as he moved toward sixty, Sinatra came to understand what Bogart meant. Certainly, when he was in New York, he sought out his favorite newspapermen. Cannon was his friend, while the rest of us were friendly

acquaintances. Cannon was only five years older than
Sinatra, a New Yorker shaped by Prohibition and the Depression, the myth of 1930s Broadway, and World War II
in Europe, where he served as a correspondent for *Stars
and Stripes*. They spoke the same language, shared passions for boxers, ballplayers, and beautiful women. Cannon brought a poetic language to his sports columns,
some of which were shaped like songs, and his essentially
romantic vision of that world was saved from sentimen-
tality by a knowing New York tone. Like Sinatra, he was
afflicted by insomnia and bouts of personal loneliness;
he read widely and intelligently, deep into the night.
Sinatra never gave up the whiskey, but he was a reader
too; he and Cannon talked at all hours of the night about
books, and it was Cannon who urged him to read Nelson
Algren's *The Man with the Golden Arm*, which was the
basis of one of Sinatra's finest movies. It didn't matter
where they were staying; insomniacs without wives can
always be reached by phone.

Cannon also got Sinatra to read Murray Kempton,
who was writing his brilliant column for the *New York
Post* in the same years that Cannon was the star of the
sports section. Kempton was an absolute original who
brought a unique, mandarin style to newspapers; on
some days it was as if Henry James had agreed to cover
the longshoremen's union. He had an extraordinary
sympathy for rascals, outcasts, those subjected to lofty
moralizing. Nobody ever wrote more intelligently about

Sinatra than Kempton did in a handful of columns across the years. But Kempton, who also liked his whiskey, was not a man who moved easily through the night. It was hard to imagine him sitting around in saloons. But Sinatra loved his work and would have his columns (and Cannon's) airmailed to him each day in California. "The man is a marvel," he said to me once about Kempton. "It's like listening to Louis Armstrong, or Roy Eldridge: you don't know where the hell he is going, but somehow he gets there and it knocks your socks off." He made certain that Kempton covered the 1961 inaugural party for John F. Kennedy, which Sinatra produced. He joined him occasionally at more formal parties in New York, sometimes at his own apartment on East Seventy-second Street, near Third Avenue. He sent him fan mail, which he signed "Francis Albert." But he didn't call much on the telephone. "Kempton is one of those guys," he explained, "that makes me feel tongue-tied."

I was twenty years younger than Sinatra, but he seemed to be comfortable when I was around. It certainly helped that Cannon and Shirley MacLaine had vouched for me, and he was impressed that I knew Kempton. There might have been one other factor: Cannon and I were both high school dropouts, as was Sinatra. (Oddly, Cannon and I had dropped out of the same institution, a great Jesuit high school called Regis.) This might have meant more to Sinatra than it did to us; in a very important way he defined success as a triumph over the odds.

"Every time they print your column," he said to me once, "you are getting your fucking diploma."

I laughed. But he was serious.

Later, Sinatra had one other newspaper friend, Sidney Zion, now a fine columnist for the *New York Daily News*. Zion came out of Paterson, New Jersey, went to law school, worked as a prosecutor, and then became a reporter for the *New York Post*. Like all of us at the paper, he worshiped Kempton. But he had been shaped by the traditions and lore of urban New Jersey. The figure of Frank Sinatra was an immense part of that tradition. Zion loved the music that Sinatra loved most, the music of the hours after midnight. He loved saloons. He loved smoking and drinking (and still does). He is a wonderful storyteller.

"I got to know him around 1980, the time of the *Trilogy* album," Zion told me. "I did a piece about the old music for the *Times*, and one thing led to another. A mutual friend introduced us, and I'd see him when he was in New York. I think he liked me because he'd never met a Jew who drank as much as I did."

Sinatra was always more cynical about the Hollywood press corps. He thought most of them were freeloaders, or on the take. "I've seen the bills, baby," he said once about reporters and columnists who took money from the publicity budgets of the studios. In his early years he had cooperated with the fan magazines and other components of the Hollywood publicity machine. At some points he had even groveled to the more powerful columnists when advised to do so (although the most powerful columnist of all, Walter Winchell, never joined in the attacks on Sinatra). But from the mid-1950s until his death, he worked with the press only on his own terms.

"The New York guys are different," he said. "Maybe because there's so much else going on around them, they don't have to cover *me*. Ah, shit, I like their company. It's as simple as that."

Maybe it was, but I doubt it.

IV. Jimmy Cannon, Murray Kempton, and William B. Williams are dead. So are Jilly Rizzo and Sugar Ray Robinson and all those others who once seemed so vividly alive that I could not imagine them leaving the world. Now Sinatra is dead too, and it's like a thousand people have just left the room.

And yet the tale of Frank Sinatra isn't only about Clarke's and Hollywood and Las Vegas; the life he led in such places is part of the tale, but it would be meaningless without the art. Sinatra's art can be experienced in the 1,307 recordings he made in studios from 1939 to 1995, in the recordings of his concerts, in his videos and movies. In the saloons of the city, you could see what

Sinatra had become. But such evenings could never explain the long existential saga of a life entwined with art. He was, in some ways, as elusive and mysterious as Jay Gatsby, not simply to those who knew him but to himself. The keys to the life and the art can only be found somewhere back in the vast obscurity beyond the city.

MANY IMMIGRANTS HAD BROUGHT ON BOARD
BALLS OF YARN, LEAVING ONE END OF
THE LINE WITH SOMEONE ON LAND. AS THE
SHIP SLOWLY CLEARED THE DOCK, THE
BALLS UNWOUND AMID THE FAREWELL SHOUTS
OF THE WOMEN, THE FLUTTERING OF THE
HANDKERCHIEFS, AND THE INFANTS HELD HIGH.
AFTER THE YARN RAN OUT, THE LONG STRIPS
REMAINED AIRBORNE, SUSTAINED BY THE
WIND, LONG AFTER THOSE ON LAND AND THOSE
AT SEA HAD LOST SIGHT OF EACH OTHER.

—LUCIANO DE CRESCENZO,
Quoted in *La Merica:*
Images of Italian
Greenhorn Experience

· 2 ·

WRAP YOUR TROUBLES
IN DREAMS

THE LIFE AND CAREER of Frank Sinatra are inseparable from the most powerful of all modern American
myths: the saga of immigration. Because he was the
son of immigrants, his success thrilled millions who
were products of the same rough history. Through the
power of his art and his personality, he became one of
a very small group that would permanently shift the image of Italian Americans. Many aspects of his character
were shaped by that immigrant experience, which often
fueled his notorious volatility. More important, it infused
his art.

"Of course, it meant something to me to be the son of
immigrants," Sinatra said to me once. "How could it not?
How the hell could it not? I grew up for a few years

thinking I was just another American kid. Then I discovered at – what? five? six? – I discovered that some people thought I was a dago. A wop. A guinea." An angry pause. "You know, like I didn't have a fucking *name*." An angrier pause. "That's why years later, when Harry [James] wanted me to change my name, I said no way, baby. The name is Sinatra. Frank fucking Sinatra."

He grew up in a time when the wounds caused by nativism and anti-Italian bigotry were still raw. Those wounds, and the scar tissue they left behind, affected the way millions of Italian Americans lived, what they talked about, even how they chose to read the newspapers. In the years of his childhood, Sinatra was no exception.

"Growing up, I would hear the stories," he said to me once. "Things that happened, because you were Italian. . . . I don't mean it was the *only* thing people talked about. That would be a lie. But the stories were there. The warnings, the prejudice. You heard about it at home, in the barbershop, on the corner. You never heard about it in school. But it was there. Later, I heard the same kinds of things from my Jewish friends, how *they* learned about the ways they could get in trouble. Always the same old shit."

The stories were about insults, exploitation, worse. Part of the trouble was caused by sheer numbers. From 1880 to the beginning of World War I, more than 24 million Europeans crossed the Atlantic to America. About 4.5 million were Italians, 80 percent of them fleeing the exhausted hills and emptying villages of Il Mezzogiorno, the neglected provinces of southern Italy and Sicily. Many thousands went to Brazil. Another million journeyed to Argentina and permanently transformed the character of that nation. The vast majority came to the United States. At first, the more adventurous Italians moved west, helping build thousands of miles of railroad tracks, finding jobs as fishermen on the sunny coasts of California or developing that state's lush vineyards. Most settled in cities.

"I read a book once about how the Irish when they came to America never wanted to be farmers again," Sinatra said. "I guess if you work on a farm and everything dies in the ground, you don't ever trust the ground again. The Italians were like that too."

Rural Italian and Irish immigrants shared that common grievance against the Old Country: the exhausted or poisoned land had failed them and, in a way, betrayed their faith and prayers; in the New World, they sought the solace of cities. Cement was better than hunger; a job and a lock on the door provided the only true safety. The Jews, haunted by the brutal realities of recurrent pogroms, or disenfranchised by a crippling, pervasive anti-Semitism, were drawn by the even brighter promise of freedom; no matter how terrible life might be in the slums of the Lower East Side, the Cossacks would not arrive at dawn with their sabers drawn. The Irish, Italian, and Eastern European Jewish immigrants shared a suspicion of government and the police that helped form the style of the American cities where they settled. Their children were touched, in various degrees, by their Old Country lore and their nostalgias. Many of Frank Sinatra's attitudes came from that mixture.

But in the last years of the nineteenth century, rural Italians faced some special problems in urban America, burdens that did not afflict the Irish and the Jews in the same way. Even in the Italian language, too many immigrants could not read or write. Depending upon the year, between 50 and 70 percent of the new arrivals were illiterate. This was a severe handicap in the booming, more complex cities of the United States and forced many into manual labor or trades that did not demand book learning. Four thousand Italian immigrants found work building the New York subways. Others labored in the building trades, helping erect the soaring monuments of twentieth-century New York. Many worked as barbers or seamstresses, as blacksmiths or mechanics or stonemasons. Some were chefs or bakers. Others were fruit and vegetable peddlers, bootblacks, or shoemakers. A few created an instant stereotype: the organ grinder. These small mustached men moved through many neighborhoods, equipped with hand organs, an occasional monkey, and a cup for coins. For most people the organ grinder was a passing amusement, singing "O Sole Mio" into the humid air of a Saturday morning; for many Italian Americans, the organ grinder was a humiliation, a beggar with a monkey and a voice.

Most of the time, the Italians did their work with silent courage and little public complaint. If you came from a place where there were never enough jobs, work itself was a kind of triumph. For those immigrants, there was no such thing as a meaningless job; the job itself was the meaning.

"They did whatever the hell they had to do to put food on the table," Sinatra said to me once. "They took any kind of dumb job, and you know why? So their *kids* wouldn't have to do those jobs. So *you* wouldn't have to do it. So *I* wouldn't have to do it. They were some kind of people."

The Italians also had to undergo another peculiarly American rite of passage: they had to endure and then confront the ferocious bigotry of those who had come before them. This was compounded by the American obsession with race. At the peak of the migration, there were millions of African Americans still alive who had lived as slaves; political compromise was leading to an iron segregation in the American South; various hare-brained race theorists spent their time sniffing out hidden racial strains in individuals. Guilt over slavery, and over the partial extermination of American Indians, created self-serving notions about the inferiority of those with darker skin. Along came the Italians. The majority of Italian immigrants were Sicilians, from an island where Arab and Spanish conquerors had been dominant for centuries. The glories of those civilizations meant nothing to many older Americans; the darker complexions of the Mediterranean were suspect among those who believed that Americans were supposed to be fairskinned. The coarse, hurting language of ethnic inferiority followed, and it affected Frank Sinatra. Even in the years of his fame and power, Sinatra could not completely insulate himself from the social cruelties of that process.

"Every once in a while," he told me, "I'd be at a party somewhere, in Hollywood or New York or wherever, and it would be very civilized, you know, black tie, the best crystal, all of that. And I'd see a guy staring at me from the corner of the room, and I knew what word was in his head. The word was *guinea.*"

Some of this social minefield was waiting for the Italians when they got off the boat at Castle Garden or Ellis Island. In the 1890s, when Frank Sinatra's grandparents made their separate passages from Italy, carrying with them the children who would become his parents, a renewed nativist fever was surging through the United States. It was driven, of course, by fear. A fear of Catholics, a fear of Jews, a fear of strange languages and secret societies, a fear of race, a fear of People Who Are Not Like Us. The Irish had gone through this paranoid test for the half century following the Great Famine that sent them to America. For a shorter period of time, the Jews who arrived on the same great immigrant tide as the Italians would suffer similar humiliations. Mexicans, Dominicans, and many Asians are today objects of the same collective stupidity. For the Italians and their children, this brutal ritual would last much longer than for other groups. And a hundred years ago it was not a simple matter of manners, social slights, or bigoted jokes. It could be a matter of life and death.

"Guys my age, one reason they didn't pay much attention to school was the schools didn't tell stories *we* knew," Sinatra said. "We heard what had happened in different places. We didn't get it from school."

One story that Sinatra heard was about an event that happened about the time his parents and grandparents arrived in the United States. In 1891 a singular atrocity took place in New Orleans that drastically altered the situation of all Italian Americans. A group of Italian immigrants were accused of murdering a corrupt police superintendent named David Hennessy. Nineteen were charged with the crime; eleven were tried for murder. There was much lurid talk in the newspapers of the day about the Black Hand, a secret gang of Sicilians dedicated to crime. Then, for the first time, many Americans heard the word *Mafia*. This was even bigger than the Black Hand. The Mafia myth, which conferred immense hidden powers to a relative handful of hoodlums, was born. It didn't matter that among the 4.5 million Italian immigrants, no more than a few thousand were connected to the Honored Society; it didn't matter that in the prisons of New York, the Italians were a tiny minority among an army of Irish lawbreakers. The myth had been spawned in New Orleans. Spreading like a stain, inflated by novels and movies and a cottage industry of hysterical politicians and prosecutors, the dark myth would affect all Italian Americans; it would directly affect the life of Frank Sinatra.

"Half the troubles I've had," he said once, "were because my name ended in a vowel. They tried to put me together with all the other stuff that happened. I wasn't the only one. But there I was, up on a goddamned stage. I was pretty easy to see, a good target."

In New Orleans the garish myth flowered in the imaginations of newspapermen. There were gangsters among us, the newspapers said, who were different from Irish gangsters or American gangsters; they were darker, swarthier, spoke a different language, and were bound together by blood oaths! In largely Catholic New Orleans, famous for its easy, tolerant ways, the myth had crude power; paranoia usually does. Even among some supporters of the Irish Republican Brotherhood, a secret society if there ever was one, it was believed that the Italians were different. The IRB wanted freedom for Ireland; the Mafia wanted *America!*

But then a strange thing happened in the New Orleans trial of the Italian immigrants for the murder of

David Hennessy: the jury acquitted eight of the men and reached no verdict on the other three. The evidence simply wasn't there. Not about this specific murder. And not about the Mafia.

That verdict did not satisfy the respectable Americans of New Orleans. They claimed the fix was in. They claimed that the shadowy Italian organization had paid off the jurors. Two days after the verdicts a mob of several thousand, led by sixty leading citizens and including a small number of African Americans, surrounded the jail where the Italians were awaiting final bureaucratic disposition of their cases. The Americans stormed the jail, dragged the Italians out of their cells, and murdered them. Two were hanged screaming from lampposts. One of them tried climbing the hangman's rope with his free hands and was riddled with bullets. Seven were executed by firing squads in the yard of the jail. Two crawled into a prison doghouse to hide from the mob, were discovered, and were shot to pieces. It remains the worst single lynching in American history.

"When I was young," Frank Sinatra said when he was in his sixties, "people used to ask me why I sent money to the NAACP and, you know, tried to help, in my own small way. I used to say, Because we've been there too, man. It wasn't just black people hanging from the end of those fucking ropes."

The story of the New Orleans outrage spread swiftly through the world of the Italian immigrant in America, underlined by the decision of the Italian government to withdraw its ambassador in protest. Mainstream America didn't express much horror. According to Professor Richard Gambino, in his book *Vendetta*, the lynchings were approved by the editorial writers of the *New York Times, Washington Post, St. Louis Globe-Democrat,* and *San Francisco Chronicle,* along with about 50 percent of the other newspapers in the nation. Theodore Roosevelt, one of the leading younger Republicans, said the lynchings were "a rather good thing" and bragged that he had said so at a party to "various dago diplomats."

"Maybe that's why so many people didn't trust the newspapers, even if they *could* read them," Sinatra said, almost eighty years later. Then he laughed. "Maybe it's why I did so many dumb things with newspapermen too."

The message from New Orleans was clear to the immigrants. Americans didn't like Italians. An American was supposed to be white, Anglo-Saxon, and Protestant. He was supposed to come from northern Europe. Yes, the Americans talked big about democracy and equality and the virtues of hard work; but in reality, the game was rigged. In the aftermath of the New Orleans lynchings, a grand jury couldn't find enough evidence to indict the murderers, in spite of the presence of hundreds of eyewitnesses. Instead, the grand jurors indicted six men who worked for the *defense* attorneys, charging them with jury tampering. This chilling illustration of the failure of the American criminal justice system was part of a wider pattern. There were anti-Italian murders in the Midwest and barn burnings on the property of Italian farmers in the American South. Men from the drought-stricken fields of Sicily and Calabria were in awe of the rich earth of La America, but too often they were driven off that land by night riders. It was no surprise that many of those once-optimistic and naive Italians sought refuge in the cities. And no surprise that their ghettos became fortresses, where only one social unit mattered: the family. Nobody else could be trusted, up to and including the president of the United States.

In such places the Mafia *did* begin to establish itself, usually victimizing Italians but bringing a kind of authority to the social structure of the ghetto. If the government treated you with contempt or suspicion, if trade unions rejected you, if at last your children had a chance for an education and the teachers made fun of them, then you would have to live by your own rules, or pack up and leave. In fact, hundreds of thousands of Italians did go home, many of them embittered by their American experience. For them, the promises implied by the Statue of Liberty were part of a cruel joke; more Italian immigrants returned home than any other nationality.

But millions stayed on, seeking their own means of protection within the warm fortress of the family and its extension, the ghetto. If, in the pursuit of justice or progress they could not depend upon the police or the courts, if they could not obtain loans from the banks, then they would go to the man in the white suit from Francis Ford Coppola's version of *The Godfather,* the agent of the Honored Society. He could arrange for extortionary loans. He could settle disputes. He could dispense rough justice. Always at a price, of course. In cash, or in obligations. During the years before World War I, he was a parochial figure, strictly local, an exotic import, a poisonous flower unique to the closed ghetto hothouse. But he was created by an American failure. More than anything else, he emphasized how cut off many Italian immigrants were from the larger American society.

This isolation, this shared solitude, created problems that took generations to solve. Education was often sneered at; what was the use of working hard in school if you couldn't take a diploma into a good job? "I know a guy went to college," I would hear from my Italian American friends growing up in Brooklyn. "He's driving a truck." Many would retreat into passivity, keeping their heads down, getting through a life in silence and safety. Others would try to defuse potential danger by performing the public role of caricatured Italian Americans, the organ grinder, the fruit peddler, a Mediterranean variation on the earlier role of the Stage Irishman.

"You know what radio show I hated the most?" Sinatra would say, many years later. "It was called *Life with Luigi,* with J. Carrol Naish — there's a good Italian name for you — and it was all about Italians who spoke like-adis, and worried about ladies who squeeze-a da tomatoes on-a da fruit stand. The terrible thing was, it made me laugh. Because it *did* have some truth to it. We all knew guys like that growing up. But then I would hate myself for laughing at the goddamned thing."

This is certain: many of the older people among whom Frank Sinatra grew up in Hoboken were shaped by the stark conflict between what America promised and what America delivered. Such a conflict can lead to the development of a defensive style, the adoption of masks of cynicism or irony, or some merger of both. Or it can lead to the guise of the don't-fuck-with-me tough guy. At different times Sinatra would try on all the masks.

"Sometimes with me, it was a case of if-you-got-the-name-you-might-as-well-have-the-game," he said to me once. "You think I'm just some wop wise guy off the street? All right, I'll *be* a wop wise guy off the street and break your fucking head."

II. For those Italians who stayed on in the American cities, life did have its consolations. In spite of the cold-water tenements, the hostile police, the sneers of strangers, the slurs in the newspapers, life in those cities was better than it was in the places left behind. As if to maintain continuity with the Old Country, the Italian immigrants – like the Irish before them – reproduced many of the rhythms of the old life. Sinatra grew up in a world of feasts, weddings, funerals, and celebrations, with insistence on the traditions of courtship, marriage, personal honor. At the same time, he was pulled by baseball, the Fourth of July, the vistas of the American deserts that were shown in westerns at the movie house. He was forced to choose between two modes of thinking, admirably described by Richard Gambino in his study *Blood of My Blood.* One was *la via vecchia,* the old way, the rules as encoded over many centuries in the Old Country. The other was *la via nuova,* the new way, the American way, with its loose rules, its many freedoms, its abundance of choices. In some important ways, Sinatra was faithful to the old way: suspicious of, if not hostile to, authority; possessive of women; needy of family. Like most young people of his age, he despised informers, thought the law was hypocritical, the world a hard place. At the same time, he was a genuine product of the new way, exulting in the freedoms of the American, gambling for big stakes in life and career, seizing all opportunities.

Walking the streets of the neighborhood, listening to the grown-ups talk at kitchen tables or in barbershops, he came to understand something else. It was called power. Within the Little Italies of the American cities, there existed subtle structures of social power, most of them carried intact from the Old Country. As Luigi Barzini has written:

"Power has many sources. The first and nearest source is one's family. In Sicily the family includes relatives as far as the third, fourth, or fifth degree, collaterals, in-laws, relatives of the in-laws, godfathers and godmothers, best men at marriages, dependents, hangers-on, servants, and vassals. They all help or must be helped, as the case may be, in times of necessity."

In the years of his own power, Frank Sinatra would remain true to that particular vision of responsibility; he was ferocious in protecting his family (even after leaving his first wife); he often acted as if it was his duty, and his alone, to come to the aid of friends when they were in trouble. In some ways, of course, this attitude was not unique to Sicilians or to Italians in general; there was a pagan or Christian element to it, as could be seen among the Irish, and a tribal or religious element that could be witnessed among Jews who came together from many nations and accepted responsibility for one another. But the style and its underlying codes made their marks on Sinatra in Hoboken.

"When I was there, I just wanted to get the hell out," he said. "It took me a long time to realize how much of it I took with me."

In Hoboken, as in other places, the story was certainly not one of unrelieved misery. The core of the immigration myth is this: it was about the way people overcame misery, how they found their consolations, and, in the end, how they redeemed America in a time when America believed it was not in need of redemption. There was a spirit of patient optimism in Sinatra's

Hoboken, although he could not have imagined as a child that he would one day become one of the agents of consolation.

For millions of Italian immigrants and their children, technology would provide some of those consolations and accelerate the process of Americanization. The rapid development of the motion picture would provide one form of national unity, allowing people from every region and every ethnic group to share common emotional experiences, some of them virtually mythic. More important, when Frank Sinatra was a child, the phonograph and the radio were invented. When each became widely available, the lives of the immigrants changed in a revolutionary way. Many immigrants added wind-up Victrolas — which came on the mass market in 1915 — to their American homes. After 1921, when regular radio broadcasting began on WJZ out of Newark, those ghetto-bound immigrants who were cut off from English could listen to it at home, trying to crack its codes, while their English-speaking children were entranced. A few years later the immigrants could listen to the Italian-language radio stations, and thus be informed and entertained even if they could not read or write in any language. An even greater impact was made upon their children. Frank Sinatra was part of a generation that could not remember a time when there was neither a radio nor a phonograph in the house; by the time of his first communion, he was listening to the music of America.

"The radio was like a religion," Sinatra remembered. "They were even shaped like cathedrals."

For the immigrants themselves, the phonograph was initially more important. For the first time, Italian immigrants could bring great music into their daily lives in ways that were impossible in the Old Country. These were people, the *contadini* from the countryside, who could never afford entrance to opera houses or grand concert halls. If they could buy the tickets, they could not afford the clothes that would grant them entry. Many knew the melodies of Puccini and Verdi from the singing of inspired amateurs. They had heard some of the music from the mouths of organ grinders. But now here was Caruso himself, singing in their kitchens or living rooms. After 1940 Frank Sinatra would also sing in many of those rooms.

III. Two immigrant couples concern us here: one from Sicily, the other from the distant north of Italy. They had a common goal but were shaped by different histories and geographies. As a nation, after all, Italy was even younger than the United States; the various city-states were not consolidated into a united Italy until 1871. To be Italian instead of Piedmontese or Sicilian required an act of the imagination so powerful that it could erase the disputes and violence of centuries. For many, that psychological unification never happened. Even in America, the old regional and city conflicts often continued, leading to snubs and feuds and rare spurts of violence; it took American bigotry to make them all feel like Italians. And by then most of them wanted to be something else: Americans. If they were not readily accepted, so be it; their children would be Americans by right of birth.

Begin with the Sicilian couple. John and Rosa Sinatra (the name, in some versions of the tale, was originally Sinestra, and "John" surely must have been baptized Giovanni) were from Agrigento, a lovely town on the southwestern coast of the island. The town was founded by the Greeks about 500 B.C. Growing up in Agrigento, the Sinatras were familiar with the extensive Greek ruins, the underground water systems built by the Greeks, the secret catacombs. There were traces, too, of centuries of occupation by the Saracens, and later by the Spanish, in the language, the cuisine, and above all, in the social structure with its elites at the narrow top and the broad, uneducated mass at the bottom.

From the hills around Agrigento, a man could stare off across the Mediterranean toward Africa. Or he could look west, toward America. The town's most famous modern citizen was the novelist and playwright Luigi Pirandello (born in 1867 in a suburb appropriately called Chaos). Pirandello was almost an exact contemporary of the elder Sinatra. With their mixture of love and hate for their island, their cynicism about authority, and a need to escape and start over, many Sicilians often must have felt like characters in search of an author.

As a young man in Agrigento, John Sinatra was a grape grower, subject to the whims of wind and weather. Much of Sicily, like almost all of the "boot" of the lower mainland, had undergone across the centuries what would now be called an ecological disaster: its forests obliterated for fuel or profit. The once-rich land turned powdery in summer, hard and unforgiving in winter. In the spring, floods transformed clay into glue. The swamps were infested with mosquitoes that spread malaria. Infant mortality was high. Doctors were rare. Education did not exist.

Like millions of other immigrants, the Sinatras were seduced by the gaudy promises of shipping agents and labor contractors and made the decision to cross the ocean. John could not read or write English (and might have been illiterate in Italian), but he surely must have believed that in America, his son, Anthony Martin Sinatra, would have a better chance at a decent life than he could ever have in Sicily. The Sinatras left for America in the last decade of the nineteenth century. They settled behind the Statue of Liberty in a town called Hoboken, a once-genteel bedroom for New York City that was being swiftly transformed by the immigrant tide into an industrial workshop. The rudeness of the German longshoremen didn't matter to the Sinatras, nor did the power of the Irish police and politicians. John soon had a job in a pencil factory, earning $11 a week. It wasn't much, but it was enough to feed his family.

The other couple in our story was the Garaventes. Unlike the Sinatras, they were city people, from Genoa, a hard northern port that, with its drydocks and piers and buildingways, looks in old drawings and photographs like the waterfront of Brooklyn. Henry James, visiting in 1890, described the "wonderful crooked, twisting, climbing, soaring, burrowing Genoese alleys" and the "sensuous optimism" of the inhabitants. Founded several centuries before the birth of Jesus, conquered and ruled at various times by the French, the Saracens, and the Austrians, the port was known for centuries as La Superba, the proud or haughty one. When I visited there twenty years ago, the narrow alleys of the old town exuded a sense of danger, even menace; but the city also contained baroque marble palaces that whispered of vanished glories. Genoa's connection to America began with Christopher Columbus, who was born there. After the discovery of America, the merchants of Genoa amassed huge fortunes in trade with the New World. But the city also fomented a rebellious spirit. It was the birthplace of two great heroes of revolutionary nineteenth-century Italian nationalism, the romantic Giuseppe Garibaldi (who once lived in Staten Island) and the idealistic Giuseppe Mazzini. Those names would also be saluted in places like Hoboken.

The Garaventes settled among the poor of Hoboken, protected from outside dangers by the rigid structure of the ghetto. The fairest of their children was Natalia, known as Dolly. In Genoa her father had been a skilled lithographer, was literate, and knew the value of an education. He quickly found work while his spouse became a midwife. In Hoboken the Garaventes worked very hard to make a traditional home for their children, a place of safety and manners and respect for older people. There was no reason why the values of the Old Country should not continue in this new country; those old rules were not unique, after all – they were common to all good people. Or so they believed.

The Garaventes surely did not anticipate the assimilating power of America, *la via nuova*, the mysterious process that combined schooling, the streets, social and political institutions, and a new set of myths, peopled by baseball players, prizefighters, and movie stars. The power of *la via nuova* would inevitably change their children into Americans.

This process was dramatized about 1912. At some point that year, the young man named Anthony Martin Sinatra met the young woman named Dolly Garavente. Aside from the neighborhood in Hoboken, they had only one thing in common: each had blue eyes. Otherwise, they were very different.

Martin was quiet, shy, virtually uneducated (one account says that he was illiterate), but marked by a somber Sicilian gravity. The family narrative, constructed years later (and thus possibly suspect, as are all family narratives), tells us that, like many children of immigrants, he had turned to the prize ring, boxing at 118 pounds under the name of Marty O'Brien. We don't know if this is true; so far, no records confirm it and there seem to be no photographs of him in boxing gear. But the use of the pseudonym makes it plausible. Certainly, Martin Sinatra would not have been the only immigrant to don a mask in order to scrape out a hard living. Assuming an Irish name was not unusual in that era of boxing; there were Jewish fighters with Irish names too; and Jim Flynn, the only man who ever knocked out Jack Dempsey, was actually named Andrea Chiariglione. One reason for the name changes is that there were not enough Irish fighters to satisfy the large number of Irish fans. The Irish were living their own American success story, moving away from the practice of the brutal sport, as doors opened to politics, police work, and the law. With his blue eyes, Martin Sinatra could pass for Irish. He certainly had no major career in the ring: he suffered from chronic asthma, had easily breakable "bad hands," and in the various Hoboken versions of his tale is usually described as a club fighter of mediocre skill.

"He could fight," Sinatra said, years later. "He used to show me in the yard, you know, how to jab, how to throw a left hook, set your feet, that kind of thing. But he never hit me. Not once. Not ever. He was a gentle man. I think he was the kind of guy who never gave anyone any crap and walked away from most of the jerks he'd meet. But if you pushed him too far, watch out."

There was nothing mediocre or reserved about Dolly Garavente. She was two years old when she came to America, and said later that she had no memories of Italy. With her blue eyes, strawberry blond hair, fair complexion, and, above all, her *attitude*, she appeared solidly American. Her confident, freewheeling style might have caused some uneasiness for her parents, epitomizing, as she did, *la via nuova*. But it made her a vivid force within that family and on the street. She managed to get through the eighth grade, a considerable accomplishment for a woman in that neighborhood in those years. She was infused with that "sensuous optimism" of the Genoese, but she was also tough, ambitious, capable of brassy vulgarity in two languages. She was very different from Martin Sinatra, and that was a surprise. In his great book *The Italians*, the writer Luigi Barzini writes:

"The private aims of southerners and northerners are, of course, more or less the same. The northerner, however, thinks that there is one practically sure way to achieve them: the acquisition of wealth, *la richezza*. Only wealth can, he believes, lastingly assure the defense and prosperity of the family. The southerner, on the other hand, knows that this can be done only with the acquisition of power, prestige, authority, fame."

After Dolly Garavente married Marty Sinatra, she combined the characteristics of north and south in the same person, becoming an Italian *and* an American. That fusion helped shape the character of her only child.

She brought to motherhood a special combination of rebelliousness and will, defying many of the codes of the old way. The marriage itself was fiercely opposed by the Garaventes. From the viewpoint of haughty Genoa, marrying a Sicilian was a step down. To marry a young man who was barely literate, who was a prizefighter, who had *tattoos:* that could not be allowed. At the same time, the Sinatras were not enthusiastic either. They had no use for people from Genoa. Such people were snobs. They thought too well of themselves. Martin should forget about this boisterous woman with the blond hair and marry a nice, quiet Sicilian girl. Both sets of parents forbade the marriage. The young people ignored them and the social codes to which they gave such immense value. This was, after all, America, not the Old Country. *La via nuova* would win out over *la via vecchia.* On February 14, 1913, Dolly and Martin eloped all the way to Jersey City and were married in City Hall. It was, of course, St. Valentine's Day, the day on which Americans celebrated romance.

Romance meant little to the Sinatras and the Garaventes. Both families were outraged. A marriage in City Hall? That was no marriage. A marriage of two Catholics had to be performed by a priest! Ignoring the cold war between the Garaventes and the Sinatras, the young couple moved into a flat in an eight-family tenement at 415 Monroe Street in Hoboken. Dolly took a job in a candy shop. Marty scrambled to make a living and found work as a boilermaker in a shipyard. If necessary, they would be self-reliant; this was America. But the general unhappiness of the two families couldn't go on. The following year, to calm their parents, Dolly and Marty got married again, this time by a priest. The second ceremony took place at home. Of course. But it was done more for the parents than for themselves, a bow to *la via vecchia.*

In an important way, Marty and Dolly – especially Dolly – were part of a bridge generation of Italian Americans, technically immigrants but confident enough as Americans to use their freedoms to discard old-fashioned conventions. If the narrative of their parents' lives had been permanently interrupted when they boarded the ships for La America, their own narratives would be lived out in that same America. For them, America was not a destination; it was a place of beginnings.

"One thing about Dolly," Sinatra said later. "She never looked back very much. She was alive today and looked forward to tomorrow. That was her. The thing about my grandparents was, they never really got over leaving the Old Country."

In 1914 their personal drama overshadowed the distant dramas of the public world. Far away in Europe, in the town of Sarajevo on the last day of July, a Serbian nationalist assassinated Archduke Ferdinand and set off the horrors of the Great War. At first, in the streets of Hoboken's Little Italy, there was interest, some anxiety, but no obvious alarm. Italy immediately declared its neutrality and would not be sucked into the charnel house until May of the following year. The young Sinatra couple didn't care. By that spring of 1915, Dolly was pregnant with the couple's first child.

The tale of that birth is essential to the almost mythic structure of the Sinatra saga. Frank Sinatra was born at home on Monroe Street on December 12, 1915. Dolly's mother was present, but her skills as a midwife were simply not sophisticated enough to manage the breech birth. A doctor was summoned. He was nervous and panicky. He used forceps to extract the baby's head, but his technique was so clumsy that the boy was permanently scarred on the face, neck, and ears. Scars were a minor concern; the immediate problem was death itself. In the midst of all the blood and pain, it first appeared that the baby was dead. He was immense – thirteen and a half pounds – but he was not breathing. Dolly's mother, Rosa, moved faster than the despairing doctor. She took the baby in her hands and held him under the cold water tap in the sink. The shocked baby began to howl. Frank Sinatra was born.

IV. Later, he would have no memory of World War I, except its ending. "People started running around banging pots and pans and shouting and singing and then drinking and feasting in the streets," he remembered. "It was one great big party."

But the years of the war and its immediate aftermath

would also affect Frank Sinatra and other Italian Americans. As it grew clearer that the United States would be sucked into the great European conflict, there was much debate about the potential loyalties of so many foreign-born citizens and residents. Every immigrant was suspect. Would the immigrants and their children fight for the United States in a European war? Would the Irish fight on the side of England against Germany? Would German Americans fight against Germany? Nativism revived, now equipped with crackpot theories about the genetic inferiority of southern Europeans, and Congress passed the first of many laws that would bring an end to immigration. D. W. Griffith's *The Birth of a Nation* was released in the summer before Sinatra's birth; it was a brilliant artistic triumph, establishing much of the syntax of the feature film, but its racism was vile and served as a powerful recruiting device for the Ku Klux Klan. The Klan in those days was not simply the enemy of blacks; it hated Jews and Catholics too, and all those immigrants from southern Europe.

The paranoid American imagination was inflamed by news of revolutions in Mexico, Ireland, and, most spooky of all, Russia. By October 1917 the Bolsheviks had taken power. In the United States, fear of communism and anarchism was added to the existing fear and contempt for the foreigner. Both communism and anarchism, after all, were "foreign" ideologies. Both were organized in secrecy and believed in the use of violence. Hadn't an

Italian anarchist from Paterson, New Jersey, assassinated
King Umberto of Italy in 1900? Weren't Italian anarchists
causing labor unrest in silk factories and textile mills
and allying themselves with the revolutionaries of the
International Workers of the World? A new version of
the "dual loyalty" debate was born; were these immigrants primarily loyal to the United States or to their un-
American ideologies?

Patriotism was soon redefined. It was no longer
enough to love the United States; to prove your American identity, you also had to hate other countries and
"foreign" ideologies. In its preparations for war, the administration of Woodrow Wilson had organized a brilliant propaganda campaign whose intention was to meld
various nationalities into one. The first enemy was the
Hun; the second was the Red. The Hun bayoneted
babies. He executed nurses. He was the enemy of democracy everywhere, and the British and French were its de-
fenders (this was news to the millions who lived in their
colonies, of course, but logic was an early casualty of the
war). Tin Pan Alley was enlisted for the duration, under
the command of George M. Cohan, who created the patriotic music that is still played to this day. When the
United States declared war on April 6, 1917, there was an
orgy of flag-waving celebration, rallies, and parades.
Even Enrico Caruso made a recording of Cohan's "Over
There." There were no songs about chasing Reds.

Frank Sinatra would remember none of this. All he

remembered was the victory parades. But the immense slaughter of the Great War had broken many things in the world. The United States would assume much greater powers, acquire more swagger, and in the eyes of many be riddled with greater hypocrisies. The Golden Door, which had welcomed so many millions of immigrants, would slam shut. Those who believed in the old way would receive no reinforcements. Now there was only the new way. And Frank Sinatra would be part of it.

FOR HOW DOES ANY MAN

KEEP STRAIGHT WITH HIMSELF

IF HE HAS NO ONE

WITH WHOM TO BE STRAIGHT?

—NELSON ALGREN,
*The Man with
the Golden Arm*

· 3 ·

LONELY TOWN

As an artist, Sinatra had only one basic subject: loneliness. His ballads are all strategies for dealing with loneliness; his up-tempo performances are expressions of release from that loneliness. The former are almost all fueled by abandonment, odes to the girl who got away. The up-tempo tunes embrace the girl who has just arrived. Across his long career, Sinatra did many variations on this basic theme, but he got into real trouble only when he strayed from that essentially urban feeling of being the lone man in the crowded city. He is at his most ludicrous in the film clip where he sings "Ol' Man River" in a white tuxedo; he is at his most self-parodic in the part of the *Trilogy* album when he addresses a hymn to himself while a celestial background choir chants,

"Sinatra! Sinatra!" Like all great stars, he was susceptible to the twin temptations of flattery and mythomania. But in the end, his finest work takes place at the midnight hour, when he tells the bartender that it's a quarter to three and there's no one in the place except you and me.

There could have been no other subject, of course, if Sinatra was to draw, like any major artist, on the emotions that he felt most deeply. Frank Sinatra was the first and only child of Dolly Sinatra. After the panic, horror, and physical damage of her son's birth, she was unable to bear any more children. So Frank grew up as a lone child in a neighborhood of large families. That special condition was to mark his psyche as surely as the doctor's forceps marked his face.

"I used to wish I had an older brother that could help me when I needed him," he said. "I wished I had a younger sister I could protect. But I didn't. It was Dolly, Marty, and me."

The first child in immigrant families is also the first American, the one who truly begins the American part of the family saga. But an only child is in a position of greater isolation than most such children; he or she has no older brothers and sisters who can serve as guides; there are no younger siblings who can benefit from hard-earned knowledge. The American child is forced to tell what he knows to strangers. That is, he must go beyond the older people in his life, and find an audience. And he (or she) must find ways to deal with the deepest loneliness: the hours after the audience is gone and the boy closes the door to his room.

"There's nothing worse when you are a kid than lying there in the dark," he said to me once. "You got a million things in your head and nobody to tell them to."

Frank Sinatra's personal solitude was compounded by the nature of his parents. His father lived much of his life in a dark pool of silence. "He was a nice guy," Sinatra said later. "I loved him. But the man was the loneliest guy I ever knew." The boy also must have been uneasy trying to separate his father, Marty Sinatra, from the public person called Marty O'Brien. A private Italian and a public Irishman. A man who was alone at a kitchen table but known publicly to dozens of people on the street. In those days it would not have been strange for a boy to believe that the man was ashamed of being Italian. His father's split identity surely explains, at least in part, Sinatra's later vehemence about keeping his own name when Harry James wanted to change it.

"He wanted me to call myself Frankie *Satin!*" he remembered many decades later, chuckling as he spoke. "Can you imagine? Is that a name or is that a name? Now playing in the lounge, ladies and gennulmen, the one an' only *Frankie Satin*. . . . If I'd've done that, I'd be working cruise ships today." He laughed, and then turned serious. "Besides, one fake name in the family was enough."

The boy (who was, by the way, christened Frank, not Francis Albert, at St. Francis Roman Catholic Church in

Hoboken on April 2, 1916) also had to deal with the absence of Dolly Sinatra. She lived at home and was house proud, but she was gone throughout most of the day, working at a chocolate shop, leaving the boy Frank in the care of his grandmother, Rosa Garavente. In the evenings Dolly's energies were increasingly absorbed by the duties and rewards of local politics.

She was a Democrat, of course, because the Republicans then, as now, were believed to be anti-immigrant but also because in that part of New Jersey, Democrats had power. She eventually became the leader of the Third Ward in Hoboken's Ninth District, able to deliver a minimum of six hundred votes to the Hudson County machine run by Boss Hague. To such political activists, ideology was much less important than the practical benefits that came from belonging to a powerful group. You could reward your friends. You could punish your enemies. Or at least hold them back. For many Italians and their children, holding off enemies was a serious matter. By the time Frank Sinatra was ten, there were millions of Ku Klux Klan members across the nation, 40,000 in New Jersey alone; a Klan branch even operated in Hoboken, under the leadership of King Kleagle George P. Apgar, and the haters in the white sheets made no secret of their contempt for Italians. Through politics, Dolly could enlist the law on the side of the Italians in her ward. But even before issues of common defense, she was absorbed with the more mundane concerns of her vocation: the granting of favors. I mentioned once to Sinatra the saying of Boss Tweed: "It's better to know the judge than to know the law."

"That could've been my mother talking," he said, and shook his head in a fond way. Alas, knowing the judge didn't help Dolly when one of her brothers was arrested in 1921 for his part in an armed robbery that left a Railway Express worker dead. He wasn't the shooter, but he drove the getaway car and was sentenced to ten to fifteen years at hard labor. It could have been worse; he could have been executed.

Even though she was seldom around, Dolly would be a permanent force in her son's life. As a very young child, Sinatra was often dressed as a girl; Dolly had wanted a girl, bought clothes for a girl, and wasn't going to waste them. As he grew older, she dressed him with pretensions toward elegance. It was necessary to honor the tradition of *la bella figura*, dressing as a form of show. There is a studio photograph of the boy at about age five, in full formal dress, with a four-in-hand white bow tie and a carnation pinned to his lapel. He is holding a top hat, one hand resting casually on the seat of a studio chair. His face is both intelligent and tentative, absorbed in the process of the photograph, looking warily at something, or someone, slightly to the left of the photographer. Probably it was Dolly Sinatra. Probably she was giving him stage directions. The photograph, after all, was not for him. It was for her.

II. It should never be forgotten that Sinatra came to con-
sciousness during Prohibition. He was four years old
when the Eighteenth Amendment went into effect at
midnight on January 16, 1920. The weather in the New
York area was bitterly cold, the temperatures down to six
degrees above zero. Many saloons arranged farewell parties, with black-bordered invitations reading "Last rites
and ceremonies attending the departure of our spirited
friend, John Barleycorn." The Noble Experiment was
about to change life in America, but not in ways its
bluenosed adherents suspected.

"Prohibition was the dumbest law in American history," Sinatra said one night. "It was never gonna work,
not ever. But what it did was create the Mob. These dum-
mies with their books and their investigations, they
think the Mob was invented by a bunch of Sicilians in
some smoky room someplace. Probably in Palermo.
Bullshit. The Mob was invented by all those self-righteous
bastards who gave us Prohibition. It was invented by
ministers, by Southern politicians, by all the usual goddamned idiots who think they can tell people how to live.
I know what I'm talking about on *this* one. I was there."

Yes, he was. From ages four to eighteen, Sinatra
watched the story of Prohibition unfold all around him,
most clearly within his own family. In his own kitchen he
heard the justifications and rationalizations for breaking
what was perceived to be an unjust law. It is no accident
that he later became a fan of *The Great Gatsby*, which

was driven by the romantic image of the bootlegger. In Hoboken (as in other immigrant communities), one of the specific rationalizations was that the Eighteenth Amendment was a betrayal of the men who fought World War I. The timing of its passage was all wrong. The Great War had succeeded in making many young Italians feel more like Americans. The draft took them out of the ghettos and allowed them to meet young men from all over the country. Some were treated harshly by isolated bigots. Most forged friendships that lasted a lifetime. There is nothing like fighting in a foreign war to erode parochialism. Italian Americans had died for their country – the United States of America. They had been wounded. They had been gassed. They had earned the right to be called Americans.

Back home, in all the Hobokens of America, those who did not become warriors succumbed to the immensely successful propaganda campaign designed by the Wilson administration to convince immigrants and their children to fight in a European war. The nativist cliché about divided loyalties made life miserable for German Americans but didn't apply to the Italian kids. In that war, Italy was an ally of the United States, and its armies fought bravely, even after the disastrous defeat at Caporetto in 1917 (one casualty on the Italian side in that fierce battle was a young American volunteer ambulance driver named Ernest Hemingway). At home, there was a prolonged fever of flag-waving, drum-beating patriotism, and Sinatra remembered hearing Caruso's recording of "Over There."

"In the parade, when the war ended, there were guys from the block, from the neighborhood," Sinatra remembered later. "They were wearing American uniforms, not Italian uniforms. When Caruso sang 'Over There,' he could have been them."

The young men of Hoboken came home with all the other Americans to find that their country was less free than when they had departed. Suspect immigrants were being rounded up and deported as the result of the Red Scare, the first of the recurrent waves of hysteria over "foreign" ideologies. Worse, the Eighteenth Amendment had been passed while the soldiers were gone. The temperance forces were triumphant, a strange alliance of Bible-whacking fundamentalists, addled nativists, women suffragists, old line WASPs. Some, as always, had good intentions but did not see that their chosen path would lead to just another kind of hell. On the street level, the Noble Experiment was widely perceived as an additional attempt to tame, or cage, the immigrants and their children; most Prohibitionists also supported harsh new restrictions on immigration, some of them (against Asians) plainly racist, the rest directed at the people of southern Europe. This was all part of a wide national reaction against the teeming American cities, which were perceived as centers of vice and immorality, filling up with too many foreigners, too many Catholics and Jews.

There were intelligent voices raised against Prohibition, saying that it was a restriction on personal liberty, which it was, and doomed to lead to widespread corruption, which it did. Many agreed with the New York madam Polly Adler, who said about enforcing these invincibly stupid laws: "They might as well try to dry up the Atlantic with a post office blotter." Madams, alas, know more about human nature than do ministers. In New York City on the eve of Prohibition, there were 15,000 places where a man could get legally drunk; within a few years there were 32,000 speakeasies providing the same service in defiance of the law. The same phenomenon was true in New Jersey. And Dolly Sinatra was to open her own speakeasy on the corner of Fourth Street and Jefferson in Hoboken. She called it Marty O'Brien's.

"It was supposed to be a restaurant," Sinatra remembered. "And you could get some pasta there, or a sandwich. But it was really a saloon. She didn't call it Mama Sinatra's, remember; she called it Marty O'Brien's. You're Irish: would you go to a place called Marty O'Brien's for the *food?*"

Years later, while delivering the Libby Zion lecture at Yale Law School, Sinatra remembered that his father worked for a while for the early bootleggers, who made their runs north to Canada to pick up shipments of whiskey. (My father took a few similar runs himself, to the depots of Lake George.) As a prizefighter, even a mediocre one, Marty Sinatra would be a natural form of muscle.

"He was one of the tough guys," Sinatra recalled. "His job was to follow trucks with booze so that they weren't hijacked. I was only three or four, but I remember in the middle of the night I heard sounds, crying and wailing. I think my old man was a little slow, and he got hit on the head. Somebody opened up his head, and he came home and was bleeding all over the kitchen floor. My mother was hysterical. After that, he got out of that business. They opened a saloon."

Dolly Sinatra was able to run that saloon because of her political connections. She was naturally gregarious, full of spirit and jokes, equipped with a bawdy sense of humor. That made her a perfect bartender. But it was her political talents that gave her the freedom to run the place itself. She spoke the natural, rushed American English of the New York area, which allowed her to communicate easily with the Irish political bosses. She had mastered a number of Italian dialects, which made her a perfect go-between in the neighborhood between baffled individuals and the agents of the state. She knew how to get a lawyer or a tax accountant or a bailbondsman. She showed up at weddings and wakes. She was generous with her personal time, repeatedly helping those neighbors who were less fortunate than the Sinatras. But she was also a realist. She had learned how the world works and looked at it clearly. Niccolò Machiavelli, the philosopher of political lucidity, would have loved Dolly Sinatra. Yes, there was a part of her that wanted the world to be better, an idealistic streak that would reach fruition during the New Deal. But in the days of Prohibition, she was more concerned with living in the world as it was. And prospering in it.

That obviously meant knowing some of the bootleggers. Not all were Italian. The Mob was not a synonym for the Mafia. It was an alliance of Jews, Italians, and a few Irishmen, some of them brilliant, who organized the supply, and often the production, of liquor during the thirteen years, ten months, and nineteen days of Prohibition. The most famous of the original Mob chieftains were Lucky Luciano, Meyer Lansky, Ben (Bugsy) Siegel, Frank Costello, and Longie Zwillman. Their alliance – sometimes called the Combination but never the Mafia – was part of the urgent process of Americanizing crime. (Sinatra, in my conversations with him, sometimes employed the word *Mob* when referring to the gangsters of the era but usually called them "the boys.") The young Italians among them believed that it was foolish to abide by the old Sicilian traditions of excluding non-Sicilians in the name of honor and respect. Luciano, after all, was from Naples, not Sicily. Those traditional notions, the strict and narrow codes of men now patronizingly called Mustache Petes, were too vague, too old-fashioned, too rigid a part of *la via vecchia*. This was America; you worked with any nationality if it was in your common interest.

Prohibition gave them that common interest. The

model for a criminal enterprise could no longer be a local racket, safely lodged within the boundaries of a
neighborhood; it had to be organized like any large capi-
talist corporation, able to cross state lines and national
frontiers. That common interest also gave the young
Mob guys enormous profits, of course, and bootlegging
provided capital for widening their interests into the
more traditional underworld enterprises of gambling
and prostitution. The overhead was high; it took a lot of
money to pay off thousands of cops, Prohibition agents,
and prosecutors. But it was better to make payoffs than
to go around shooting guns like a bunch of cowboys.
Murder had to be an absolutely last resort; wild shooting sprees would only bring down the heat. If the scene
was peaceful, you only had to get the law to look the
other way, and that was a simple matter of paying off the
politicians.

"You know what we all thought growing up?" Sinatra
said. "We thought *everybody* was on the take. We *knew*
the cops were taking. They were right in front of us. But
we thought the priests were on the take, the schoolteach-
ers, the guy in the marriage license bureau, everybody.
We thought if God came to New Jersey, he'd get on line
to get his envelope."

In New Jersey the most important members of this
confederacy were Waxey Gordon (Irving Wexler) and
Abner (Longie) Zwillman. Years later there were people
in Hoboken who claimed that Gordon was a regular in

Marty O'Brien's. But Sinatra once told me, "The first time I ever saw his face was in a newspaper, when he got out of jail in the 1950s. He was an old man then." Still, his name was known; he controlled many rackets in Philadelphia and most of the liquor supplies in Hudson and Bergen Counties, and he had even established stills around Hoboken to manufacture beer. "Sometimes the stink was unbelievable," Sinatra remembered. "The hops, I guess. Whatever it was, it made you gag."

Zwillman was much more important than Gordon, who always deferred to him. Tall, young (born in 1899), and tough, Zwillman affected an urbane public image. His base was Newark, where he was born and served an apprenticeship as a numbers runner. He helped set up overland routes through New Jersey, assembled a fleet of thirty ships to pick up booze in Canada for delivery along the Jersey Shore, and standardized distribution in the cities. If he needed muscle, he turned to an associate named Willie Moretti, sometimes known as Willie Moore. In the early years of Prohibition, muscle was most often needed to convince the Mustache Petes that their time was over. Some were persuaded to retire. Others were shot in the head. In New Jersey this work was usually left to Moretti and his enforcement squad of about sixty men. By the time Frank Sinatra was ten, the rackets in New Jersey had settled into a routine business. Years after the end of Prohibition, Willie Moretti would play a role in the Sinatra saga too.

III. Against the cynical backdrop of Prohibition, Frank Sinatra was on his own. On the street the most admired men were tough guys. The bootlegger could be seen as a glamorous rebel, one who reaped the rewards of fine clothes, shiny cars, and beautiful women. At the movies the heroes were often cowboys, silent men, handy with guns, who rode in and out of town alone. Each taught the lesson that one solution to perceived injustice was violence. The outlaw, the desperado, the good man who was dealt a bad hand by life: they were central to the emerging American myth, as defined and spread by the new technology of mass culture.

That culture was also forming young Frank Sinatra. In 1927, a few months before Sinatra's twelfth birthday, the first talkie was released, *The Jazz Singer,* with Al Jolson. There on the screen, a man opened his mouth and you could hear him sing. The story itself was a Jewish version of the conflicts in Hoboken. Jolson played the young son of immigrants who resists his parents. They want him to sing only in synagogues; he goes out into the world and finds his way to show business, fame, and fortune. Translated into the struggles of Little Italy, it was a triumph of *la via nuova* over *la via vecchia.*

At the movies Sinatra began to dream his own American dream. Sometimes he carried those visions to school. Sometimes they were with him after school, when he was in the care of his maternal grandmother, Rosa Garavente. Old-timers from Hoboken would remember him later as a lonely boy, standing in the doorway of his grandmother's building, watching life go by without him. In a neighborhood of large families, he was often all by himself. Meanwhile, Dolly worked and laughed at the bar of Marty O'Brien's and combed the tenements for votes. The year 1927 was momentous: Lindbergh flew the Atlantic, Babe Ruth hit 60 home runs, Sacco and Vanzetti were executed in Massachusetts, Stalin took power in the Soviet Union, and Dolly Sinatra got her husband a job with the Hoboken fire department. Later, there were stories claiming that Dolly also had a side business: providing abortions. Like many families, the Sinatra family had its own secrets, and it's unlikely that they were shared with their son.

"Sometimes I'd be lying awake in the dark and I'd hear them talking," he remembered years later. "Or rather, I'd hear her talking and him listening. Mostly it was politics or some worthless neighbor. I remember her ranting about how Sacco and Vanzetti were framed. Because they were Italians. Which was probably true. All I'd hear from my father was like a grunt. They never talked about themselves. Except for things like, How could you *do* a thing like that? That was my mother. He'd just say, Eh. Eh." Sinatra smiled and said to himself, "Eh."

It was his mother he remembered most vividly. In his sixties he would remember Dolly nagging him about the dangers of tuberculosis, insisting that he stay away from kids who coughed. He remembered her fears of polio, shared by millions in those days, and her refusal to let him go to beaches or public swimming pools. (He went anyway.) He remembered how she wanted him to go on to a career as an engineer at the Stevens Institute of Technology. And he remembered how she kept a small bat, a kind of billy club, behind the bar at Marty O'Brien's.

"When I would get out of hand," he said, "she would give me a rap with that little club; then she'd hug me to her breast." He paused, and smiled: "I married the same woman every time."

He was serious. In various ways, in spite of admirable efforts to change himself and leave behind his personal disguises, Sinatra would swing back and forth between father and mother for the rest of his life. Too often he could fall into the patterns of the mute Marty Sinatra, locking himself in cramped cages of solitude. At other times he would become a male version of the garrulous Dolly, waving her vulgarity like a flag of triumph. Across his long life those swings in mood and style would offer him little relief from the template cut in Hoboken. Always he would be driven by the solitary's longing to be reconciled with the world.

On October 19, 1929, the world abruptly shifted again as the stock market crashed and the end came for what Westbrook Pegler later called the Era of Wonderful Nonsense. At first, nothing affected the neighborhood in

Hoboken or the growing prosperity of the Sinatras. Not many people in that neighborhood had plunged hard-earned money into the stock market. Some didn't even trust banks. For a while life went on. In 1930 the Sinatras moved to a three-bedroom apartment in a large house, and for the first time fourteen-year-old Frank had his own room. Now he had friends too, from the street and from David E. Rue Junior High School, where he was an intelligent but lazy or indifferent student. He seemed desperate to make friends, to be thought of as someone other than a spoiled skinny kid, someone other than Dolly's, or Marty's, son. He would play class clown. He showed a talent for drawing. (He would do much painting in the last fifteen years of his life.) He would try to buy friendship with the generous allowance money given to him by Dolly, splurging on candy, ice cream sodas, baseball gloves and bats. Contrary to the public relations myth, he was never a member of an adolescent street gang, but he did get into some fistfights. He rode a bike. He played ball. He discovered girls, developed crushes on a few, was sometimes embraced and more often rejected, with some girls making fun of the scars he'd carried from birth.

"I had some fun there," he said later, about Hoboken. "I had some misery too."

There was much misery in the land now, and it was spreading. Hoovervilles began appearing along the New Jersey and New York waterfronts, clusters of crude shacks that housed the Depression homeless. In 1931, with 4 million Americans now unemployed, there were reports of food riots in Oklahoma and Arkansas and a riot over jobs in Boston. Through all of this, Frank Sinatra was sitting in the dark, watching James Cagney hit Mae Clarke in the face with a grapefruit in *The Public Enemy* and Bela Lugosi sucking blood in *Dracula.* He no doubt talked with his friends about Al Capone going to prison for tax evasion and Legs Diamond being shot to death in a hotel room in Albany; his youth was lived in the great era of the tabloid newspaper. But he wasn't sure how he fit in. Anywhere.

"I'd rather do time in Attica than be fifteen again," he once said. "I didn't know whether I was coming or going."

That year of 1931 the Sinatras moved again, this time into their own home, which they bought for $13,400, a considerable sum in that Depression year. They had, at last, their piece of the American earth. No more paying rent. No more hassles with landlords. Now they had a three-story home at 841 Garden Street, complete with steam heat, a bathtub, and a finished basement. A house that rode high over the street. Dolly was more active politically than ever before, operating as the ward boss. She helped the Depression casualties as best she could, laying out spreads of food, trying to find work for those who had lost their jobs. She tried to persuade some despairing Italians that they should not go home, that Benito Mussolini had not created paradise in his Fascist Italy;

some departed anyway. During this period Frank Sinatra began to invent his dream.

"I was always singing as a kid," he said. "But it was never serious. I'd sing at the bar, you know, and get a round of applause, led by Dolly. There was a player piano in the joint, with music on a roll. I'd sing and they'd give me a hand, and sometimes a nickel or a quarter. It wasn't that I was so great. Mainly, they cheered because I could remember the words."

But in Dolly's saloon the only child was discovering that he needed an audience. If his mother whacked him and then hugged him, then he would present himself to strangers. If he was good, if he could be more than just a kid who remembered the words, they certainly wouldn't whack him. Their cheers would make him feel valuable, and connected to others. Maybe then Marty and Dolly would recognize his existence in some new way, and if they didn't, the hell with it. In junior high school he joined the glee club. He listened constantly to the radio, bought sheet music (he never learned to read music), and memorized lyrics. He was given a ukulele by his mother and would play and sing with his friends on the street. At the movies, he saw that singers always got the girl. On the radio he heard Rudy Vallee and Russ Columbo and Dick Powell. And then he discovered Bing Crosby.

"The thing about Bing was, he made you think you could do it too," Sinatra said, half a century later. "He was so relaxed, so casual. If he thought the words were getting too stupid or something, he just went buh-ba, buh-ba, booo. He even walked like it was no effort. He was so good, you never saw the rehearsals, the effort, the *hard work*. It was like Fred Astaire. Fred made you think you could dance too. I don't mean just me. I mean millions and millions of people. You saw Fred dance, you heard Bing sing, and it was like you were doing it. After a movie you saw guys in the street dancing. You heard them singing to their girls. It was amazing, what those men did, Bing and Fred. Some people, they danced and sang right through the fucking Depression. Every time Bing sang, it was a duet, and you were the other singer."

Young Frank Sinatra began to develop a theatrical personality to go with his singing. His mother arranged for credit at a clothing store, and he soon had so many pairs of slacks that he was nicknamed Slacksey O'Brien. He owned a phonograph and a growing collection of records. When he was sixteen, his father allowed him to use the family Chrysler, and he would take his friends for rides, often wandering as far as Atlantic City. The new house even had the ultimate luxury: a telephone. Frank Sinatra did not have a hard Depression.

"We never went hungry," he said later. "It wasn't luxury, but it wasn't bad."

He began to live a split life. On the street he donned the mask of the wise guy, an image fed by the gangster films that had taken the place of westerns in creating the myth of the American outsider. He posed like Cagney, like Edward G. Robinson. He dressed "sharp." He jingled change in the pockets of his slacks. He cursed. He talked tough. He showed his friends he would fight if he had to, and what he lacked in street-fighting talent, he made up for with courage. On the street he was developing an act, a disguise that would protect him from the world while asserting his presence in his own small piece of that world.

Alone, he was conceiving a different vision, and it had nothing to do with the neighborhood streets of Hoboken. As a teenager, he must have realized that loneliness might be his lot, but even then he refused to accept it as inevitable. Across a lifetime he would make many attempts to relieve loneliness, submerging it in marriages and love affairs, hard-drinking camaraderie, bursts of movement and action and anger, but the only thing that ever permanently worked was the music. And when he was an adolescent, a combination of words and music began to create the vision of escape. From solitude. From obscurity. From the polarities represented by Marty and Dolly Sinatra. Sometimes he would wander down to the waterfront alone, past the Hoovervilles, past the rusting tracks of the railroad spurs, out to the edge of the piers. There, he would gaze across the harbor at New York, the spires of its skyline rising toward the sky.

THE BIRTH OF A CREATURE OF HUMAN
FANTASY, A BIRTH WHICH IS A STEP ACROSS
THE THRESHOLD BETWEEN NOTHING
AND ETERNITY, CAN ALSO HAPPEN SUDDENLY,
OCCASIONED BY SOME NECESSITY.
AN IMAGINED DRAMA NEEDS A CHARACTER
WHO DOES OR SAYS A CERTAIN
NECESSARY THING; ACCORDINGLY THIS
CHARACTER IS BORN AND IS
PRECISELY WHAT HE HAD TO BE.

—LUIGI PIRANDELLO, 1925

■   ■   ■

"WHAT THE FUCK WAS THAT?"

—BENNY GOODMAN,
his back to the audience
at the New York Paramount,
as Frank Sinatra made his
entrance and the fans roared,
December 30, 1942

· 4 ·

THE SONG IS YOU

HIS FINEST ACCOMPLISHMENT, of course, was the sound. The voice itself would evolve over the years from a violin to a viola to a cello, with a rich middle register and dark bottom tones. But it was a combination of voice, diction, attitude, and taste in music that produced the Sinatra sound. It remains unique. Sinatra created something that was not there before he arrived: an urban American voice. It was the voice of the sons of the immigrants in northern cities – not simply the Italian Americans, but the children of all those immigrants who had arrived on the great tide at the turn of the century. That's why Irish and Jewish Americans listened to him in New York. That's why the children of Poles in Chicago, along with all those other people in cities around the nation, listened to him. If they did not exactly sound like him, they *wanted* to sound like him. Frank Sinatra was the voice of the twentieth-century American city.

In life even the mature Sinatra would sometimes speak in the argot of the street. He could be profane, even vulgar. The word *them* could become *dem,* and *those* could become *dose.* It depended on the company. But in the songs the diction was impeccable. The children of the Italians, the Irish, and the Jews wanted to believe that they could express themselves that way, and many of them did. In my Brooklyn neighborhood, many of us understood that we were not prisoners of the Brooklyn accent, *because* Sinatra's singing refused to use it. And he was like us. His diction was something that Sinatra learned early, from the movies.

"I'd go to the movies, and hear the leading man speaking English – not just Cary Grant, but Clark Gable and all the other guys – and I knew that my friends and I were talking some other version of the language," he said once. "So I started becoming, in some strange way, bilingual. I talked one kind of English with my friends. Alone in my room, I'd keep practicing the other kind of English."

His taste in music was formed early. He grew up listening to and memorizing the words and music of the great popular composers and lyricists of the first forty years of the twentieth century. These included Jerome Kern, Rodgers and Hart, Cole Porter, Harold Arlen, and

Johnny Mercer, to mention only a few of this extraordinary generation. Many were themselves part of the immigrant saga. Arthur Schwartz was the grandson of a buttonmaker from Russia. Harry Warren was the child of immigrants from Italy. Yip Harburg's parents were from Russia. Irving Berlin, author of "God Bless America" and a thousand other tunes, was himself an immigrant from Siberia. All were very American, creators of most of those songs that became known as the "standards" of twentieth-century American music.

As the reigning citizens of Tin Pan Alley, they wrote music for the Broadway theater. They wrote for musical revues. They wrote for the movies. Above all, they were city people, and their audiences were composed of city people. Often building on forms derived from African American rhythms, adapting European melodic structures and harmonies, the best of their music was full of wit, regret, insouciance, and sly humor. During Prohibition the music celebrated good times and a sophisticated hedonism, becoming the unrecorded sound track of the speakeasies. When the Depression hit, there was a chastened undertone to the music, a feeling of rue (as there was in the late writing of Scott Fitzgerald). Some writers were capable of biting social commentary, as in Harburg's "Brother, Can You Spare a Dime?" Most of the time, the attitude was less direct. Perhaps the apocalypse was here, the songs declared; if so, let's dance. That music was absorbed by the men and women of an entire generation. Sinatra was one of them, but he had begun to hear the music in a new way.

He heard it through the diverse filters of the streets of Hoboken, his own childhood, his personal solitude, and above all through the masculine street codes forged in the years of Prohibition. When the Noble Experiment ended on December 5, 1933, Americans didn't revert in the morning to the kind of people they were before Prohibition started; they had emerged from the era a lot more cynical and a lot tougher, qualities that would get many of them through the Depression. Sinatra applied some of those attitudes to his music.

If love lyrics were too mushy, he could sing them and make wised-up fun of the mush, and still, in some part of the self, acknowledge that there was some truth to the words. He could be tender and still be a tough guy. Ruth Etting could sing her weepy torch songs, but for men, whining or self-pity was not allowed; they were forbidden by the male codes of the city. Sinatra slowly found a way to allow tenderness into the performance while remaining manly. When he finally took command of his own career, he perfected the role of the Tender Tough Guy and passed it on to several generations of Americans. Before him, that archetype did not exist in American popular culture. That is one reason why he continues to matter; Frank Sinatra created a new model for American masculinity.

Sinatra was not, of course, a jazz singer, but his process resembled the way many jazz musicians worked. The best of them listened *creatively* to the tunes of Tin Pan Alley but heard them through the filter of their own experience, which was dominated by being black in segregated America. They transformed those songs, edited them, reinvented them, found something of value in even the most banal tunes. The instrument didn't matter. Over the years Louis Armstrong and Miles Davis found something different in the same tunes; so did Clifford Brown and Dizzy Gillespie, Lester Young and Ben Webster, Coleman Hawkins and Dexter Gordon. They understood the specific lyrics of what had become known as American standards and the general intentions of the songs; they insisted on making them more interesting as *music,* more authentic, more personal, finding a subtle core that more closely resembled the blues. The results could be entertainment, a transient diversion from the hardness of life; but the songs could be art, too, digging deep into human pain and folly. They could also be both. But these musicians approached the music with a seriousness that was pure. Sinatra worked in a similar way. He didn't play trumpet, trombone, saxophone, or piano; he rarely composed music or wrote lyrics; but he did function as a musician.

"I discovered very early that my instrument wasn't my voice," he said to me once. "It was the microphone."

II. In the tradition of the Old Country, Frank Sinatra served a long apprenticeship. He seems to have conceived the notion of being a professional singer when he was fifteen. Again, the instinct to create legend or myth obscures the facts, and not even Sinatra was a reliable witness to his own beginnings, and he knew it.

"Sometimes I think I know what it all was about, and how everything happened," he said one rainy night in New York. "But then I shake my head and wonder. Am I remembering what really happened or what *other* people think happened? Who the hell knows, after a certain point?"

One thing that really happened was the discovery that he actually did have a voice and could sing. I reminded him once of the story that Rocky Marciano, the old undefeated heavyweight champion, used to tell. He said that when he first knocked out a man in a gymnasium when he was a kid, it was like discovering he could sing opera.

"Hey," Sinatra said, "when I first realized I could sing a song, I felt like I'd just knocked out Jack Dempsey."

But in Hoboken in 1930 there were dozens of young men (and surely a few women) who could sing well. They could carry a tune. They could remember the words. Few of them thought they could become stars. That required an act of the imagination, the kind of gleaming vision that is often unique to artists, along with the type of will that is sometimes mistaken for arrogance. Above all, it took guts. To walk out of the safety of the parish is never easy; to do so during the Depression was an act of either foolishness or courage. And yet a small number of people chose to go out and try to make it in America, no matter what the odds against them.

"There really was nothing to lose," Sinatra said later. "Yes, you might fall on your ass. But so what? You could always work on the docks or tend bar. What was important was to *try.*"

The lure of big-time success was underlined by the grinding horrors of the Depression. Crime was one way out; with audacity and a gun, a kid might become a big shot. But talent was another. By the early 1930s the radio and the phonograph record, along with sound movies, were creating the first national pop singing stars. One was Russ Columbo, who had a light operatic voice and made an immense hit of "Prisoner of Love." He showed that an Italian American could be accepted beyond the boundaries of the parish, but his career was cut short in 1934 by his accidental death while cleaning an antique pistol. Rudy Vallee was another early star. But his voice was light and tremulous, he looked a bit goofy, and in personal appearances he used a megaphone; he couldn't play college sophomores forever. In the cities of the Northeast there weren't many college sophomores to identify with him anyway. Certainly kids like Frank Sinatra never wanted to grow up to be Rudy Vallee. But Bing Crosby was an altogether different model.

"You can't imagine now how big Crosby was," Sinatra said in the 1970s. "He was the biggest thing in the country. On records. On the radio. In the movies. Everybody wanted to be Bing Crosby, including me."

Crosby did understand the microphone — and the camera. He knew he didn't have to hit the second balcony with the belting style forced upon Broadway singers. The microphone permitted a more intimate connection with the audience. He didn't have to italicize his acting in movies, the way theater-trained actors did; the close-up allowed him to be natural. Crosby was relaxed, casual, and very American.

The story of Sinatra's inspiration by Crosby has been told in all the biographies: how he would sing along with the records, and how one night in 1935 he took his best girl, a dark-haired beauty named Nancy Barbato, to the Loew's Journal Square theater in Newark to see Crosby in a live appearance. On the way home he said to her, "Someday, that's gonna be me up there."

Nancy Barbato, the seventeen-year-old daughter of a plastering contractor, was skeptical; on an average Saturday night that year, about a million young American males must have been saying roughly the same thing. But Frank Sinatra had begun to believe in his own possibilities. This was America, wasn't it? And in America anything was possible. So he watched Crosby and listened to him, simultaneously opening himself to other kinds of music too. Crosby's stardom obviously inspired

Sinatra, but in the deepest, most substantial ways, his musicianship did not (the truest heirs to the Crosby singing style were Perry Como and Dean Martin). The most important and enduring influence on the young Frank Sinatra was swing music.

Beginning with Benny Goodman's breakout in the mid-1930s, and steadily gathering force, this jazz-inspired big band music was soon cutting across all racial and ethnic lines, becoming *the* music of the generation dominated by the children of immigrants. The growth of radio as a national medium accelerated this process: white kids could hear Count Basie or Duke Ellington; black kids could listen to Goodman (who included black musicians Lionel Hampton and Teddy Wilson in the band); kids of all ethnic backgrounds, including Japanese and Mexican Americans, formed their own swing bands. So although Sinatra was not directly influenced by jazz, he did become the most enduring singer to emerge from the era of the big bands, which could not have existed without jazz. Their powerful, driving, *confident* sound was emerging at the same time that Sinatra began to sing for audiences.

"I used to sing in social clubs and things like that," he told the British writer Robin Douglas-Home in 1961. "We had a small group. But it was when I left home for New York that I started singing serious. I was seventeen then, and I went around New York singing with little groups in roadhouses. The word would get around that there was a kid in the neighborhood who could sing. Many's the time I worked all night for nothing. Or maybe I'd sing for a sandwich or cigarettes – all night for three packs. But I worked on one basic theory – stay active, get as much practice as you can."

The family resisted. Marty was furious when Frank dropped out of high school in his senior year. He predicted that his son would be a bum. Dolly once threw a shoe at him in his room, expressing contempt for his dreamy ambitions; the shoe hit a photograph of Bing Crosby. Such reactions were not unique to the Sinatra family; many immigrant Catholic families discouraged the artistic ambitions of their children, for decent reasons: they did not want them to be disappointed and hurt. It was safer to take the cop's test or acquire a real trade. Among the Irish, we called this the Green Ceiling; it was enforced by the question, Who do you think you are?

When it was clear that her son was serious, Dolly gave in, paying $65 to get him a sound system that included a microphone. This was the equivalent of buying a trumpet for Miles Davis. Frank Sinatra had his instrument at last. Almost immediately, the gear made it easier for him to find places to play: amateur contests, bars, high school graduations. The Sinatra legend includes the tale of the formation of the Hoboken Four, winning first prize in 1935 on a popular radio show called *Major Bowes' Original Amateur Hour*. The winning group went off together on a Major Bowes tour. For the first time, Sinatra was being paid to sing. He and the rest of the group cut up $75 a week.

"We had turned pro," he said later. "Bowes was the cheapest son of a bitch in America, and a lowlife besides, but we were singing for money."

With Major Bowes in command, the Hoboken Four traveled all the way to California, an enormous journey for kids whose world until then had been limited to Atlantic City to the south, New York across the water, and the towns and roads of northern New Jersey. Frank Sinatra was seeing America, which until then was something he had only read about or had seen in the movies. And he was hearing swing bands on the radios in every town.

"A lot of it was crummy hotel rooms, buses, and trains," he said later. "But still, you saw how goddamned *big* the country was. And you could hear the same music everywhere. Bing, of course. But also Benny Goodman, Tommy Dorsey. You heard them more than you ever heard the national anthem. *They* were America."

The Hoboken Four did not survive the journey; they broke up soon after their return. But Frank Sinatra kept moving, working part-time as a plasterer (for Nancy's father), unloading crates of books for a wholesaler, catching rivets in a shipyard, ending up in 1937 as a singing waiter in a place called the Rustic Cabin in Englewood, directly across the Hudson River from midtown Manhattan. The pay was $15 a week, plus tips, but the newly completed George Washington Bridge led right over the river to Manhattan, the city of dreams.

The management could not afford a big band to play the music the rest of America was hearing. But Frank Sinatra was singing. Those who later claimed to have seen him at the Rustic Cabin could fill Yankee Stadium. But one who did see him was the trumpet player Harry James, who had just formed his own swing band after leaving Benny Goodman. He needed a boy singer. James heard Sinatra singing on one of the many radio shows that used him, unsponsored programs for which the singer was not paid (or, received 75 cents a performance). He decided to drive over to the Rustic Cabin for a look. Among other songs, Sinatra performed his version of "Begin the Beguine," a big hit for Artie Shaw. James was impressed, explaining later, "I liked Frank's way of talking a lyric." He gave Sinatra the job. That was the turning point, and without changing his name to Frankie Satin, the young man was on his way.

A few months earlier, on February 4, 1939, he had celebrated a raise from the Rustic Cabin to $25 a week by marrying Nancy Barbato in Our Lady of Sorrows in Jersey City. They moved into an apartment on Audubon Avenue in the same city. Frank Sinatra would never live in Hoboken again.

Now earning $75 a week, Sinatra took Nancy on the road with the Harry James orchestra. Every night he would hear James play "You Made Me Love You," his big hit with Goodman. Every night he would listen to swing music that ripped and roared, a rallying music in a bad time, and then ask questions of the musicians. How did *that* sound happen? On this record, what is *this* instrument? He was acquiring theory and practice.

The young musicians in the James band traveled all over the country, doing one-night stands, eating poorly, sleeping on buses, sometimes even returning to New York for gigs at Roseland. By all accounts, Frank Sinatra was a happy young man. He had found the family he was looking for, with his wife at the center. It was a family of men bound together by music, with ambitions far beyond the narrow goals of the streets of Hoboken. Nobody in this itinerant family dreamed of gaining lifetime employment in a shipyard or joining a New Jersey fire department.

"With Harry, for the first time in my life I was with people who thought the sky was the limit," he said to me later. "They thought they could go to the top, and that's what they aimed for. They didn't all make it, but what the hell. They knew the only direction was up."

On July 13, 1939, he went into a recording studio for the first time and made two recordings with the James band: "From the Bottom of My Heart" and "Melancholy Mood." A month later he recorded "My Buddy" and "It's Funny to Everyone but Me." Then in September he recorded "Here Comes the Night" and a song by Jack Lawrence and Arthur Altman called "All or Nothing at

All." The first release of the last song sold 8,000 copies. A few years later, after he was established as a star, it would be re-released during a musicians' strike and sell a million. On the earliest recorded vocals with the James band, Sinatra sounds uncertain, unformed, but he does have a distinctive voice. It is certainly not another imitation of Crosby. But on each succeeding date, he gets closer to what he will become, expressing the feeling of loneliness in a new way, within the context of a modern swing band. Those earliest records are like talented first drafts of a good first novel.

Near the end of the year, after only six months with James, Sinatra got an even bigger break: Tommy Dorsey came calling. The Dorsey orchestra was considered the smartest, toughest, hippest of the white swing bands. Some made the same case for Goodman, of course, calling him the King of Swing, but the argument for the Dorsey band was based on its flexibility. Both could do pulsing, vibrant, riff-driven swing pieces; Dorsey could also handle smooth ballads, which Goodman did not do well. (Most musicians of the era thought that the Glenn Miller sound was safe, mechanical, corny.) Dorsey was himself a fine trombone player, in a sweet legato style; he employed first-rate arrangers, such as Sy Oliver (from the Jimmie Lunceford band), Axel Stordahl, Bill Finegan, and Paul Weston, and superb musicians, including the trumpet player Bunny Berigan, whose talent was legendary but who would soon be destroyed by alcohol. Sinatra had inadvertently auditioned for Dorsey several years before he landed the job with Harry James. He showed up to audition for a swing band led by a man named Bob Chester. He later told Douglas-Home what followed:

"I had the words on the paper there in front of me and was just going to sing when the door opened and someone near me said, 'Hey, that's Tommy Dorsey!' He was like a god, you know. We were all in awe of him in the music business. Anyway, I just cut out completely — dead. The words were there in front of me, but I could only mouth air. Not a sound came out. It was terrible."

Sinatra didn't get the job with Bob Chester. But near the end of 1939 Tommy Dorsey's star vocalist, Jack Leonard, quit after a dispute, went off on his own, did poorly, and was eventually drafted. The war in Europe was already four months old, tensions were increasing in the western Pacific, and the United States was getting ready for its own inevitable entry into the war, twenty years after young Frank Sinatra saw those triumphant victory parades in Hoboken. Dorsey had heard the Harry James records (Jack Leonard, in fact, had played "All or Nothing at All" for him) and sent for Sinatra.

"The first thing he said was, 'Yes, I remember that day when you couldn't get out those words.'"

Dorsey signed him to a long-term contract for $125 a

week, which Sinatra needed since Nancy was now pregnant with their first child. But it wasn't easy to leave Harry James. The handsome, mustached trumpet player also had a contract with Sinatra, but he was a decent man; he knew his own band wasn't making money and that Dorsey, a "rich" band, could pay the young singer steadily and well. He tore up his contract and wished Sinatra all the luck in the world. They were still friends when James died in 1983.

"That night the bus pulled out with the rest of the boys at about half-past midnight," Sinatra later told Douglas-Home. "I'd said goodbye to them all, and it was snowing, I remember. There was nobody around and I stood alone with my suitcase in the snow and watched the taillights disappear. Then the tears started and I tried to run after the bus."

He didn't catch it. The James band went to play a gig in Hartford, and Sinatra took a train to New York. From there he went off to three years of school at Dorsey University. Every night he listened to, and learned from, some of the best musicians in the country: pianist Joe Bushkin, drummer Buddy Rich, Berigan and his replacement as lead trumpet, Ziggy Elman (a defector from the Goodman band). Sy Oliver taught Sinatra how to ride or glide over the rhythm base of a tune, not repeat it in his vocals, which was a kind of musical redundancy. Like Sinatra, these musicians had all been formed by Prohibition and the Depression, and the new vocalist liked their

style. They were hard-drinking, tough-talking, and dedicated to the music. They smoked cigarettes. They chased
women. They gambled. They cursed. And they played at
the top of their talent, or were sent packing by the re-
morseless Dorsey.

Sinatra started as one of the Pied Pipers, the band's
singing group, whose female star was Jo Stafford. She
later remembered Sinatra, walking on stage for the first
time, as "a very young, slim figure with more hair than
he needed. We were all sitting back — like, 'Oh, yeah, who
are you?' Then he began to sing." After four bars Stafford
knew that she had better listen closely. She thought,
"Wow! *This* is an absolutely new, unique sound." As she
elaborated later: "Nobody had ever sounded like that. In
those days most male singers' biggest thing was to try
and sound as much like Bing as possible. Well, he didn't
sound anything like Bing. He didn't sound like anybody
else that I had ever heard."

Sinatra swiftly gained the respect of the other members of the band, even those who were friends of the departed Jack Leonard. He had a variety of troubles with
Buddy Rich, a loner who considered himself the band's
feature attraction, with some reason (many consider him
the greatest white drummer of the century). Sinatra even
heaved a water pitcher at Rich backstage, sending shards
of broken glass scattering and splashing Stafford. But
they were also friends, rooming together on the road,
where Sinatra would absorb Rich's knowledge of rhythm

and tempo. As his confidence grew, Sinatra strengthened and refined his technique by listening to all the musicians, but above all to Dorsey. And he made records with the band. The first two were recorded on February 1, 1940 ("The Sky Fell Down" and "Too Romantic"); eighty-one others would follow.

It wasn't always easy. The son of a music teacher, Dorsey was Irish, tough, something of a martinet. A few years earlier he had fought with his older brother, Jimmy, another fine musician, and broke up their band to go off on his own. Tommy built his own orchestra into a commercial and artistic success through a combination of will and musicianship. He built his sound around his own sweet trombone playing, as exemplified by his theme, "I'm Getting Sentimental Over You," but also willingly turned the spotlight over to soloists and vocalists. He insisted on perfection from the band members and had no tolerance for the unkempt semi-bohemian styles that many musicians affected. He wanted his men to be clean-shaven and even held inspections before gigs. For the most part, the men responded; the members of the Dorsey band swaggered a bit, convinced of their superiority over other bands. But Dorsey, like Buddy Rich, was also a loner. That quality obviously touched Sinatra in ways that had nothing to do with music.

"Tommy was a very lonely man," Sinatra told Douglas-Home. "He was a strict disciplinarian with the band — we'd get fined if we were late — yet he craved company after the shows and never really got it. The relationship between a leader and the sidemen, you see, was rather like a general and privates. We all *knew* he was lonely, but we couldn't ask him to eat and drink with us because it looked too much like shining teacher's apple."

Sinatra remembered finally asking Dorsey to have dinner with him and another musician; Dorsey agreed and was touchingly grateful. "After that," Sinatra said, "he was almost like a father to me." Dorsey would, in fact, be godfather to Sinatra's daughter Nancy. During these three years Sinatra absorbed many lessons from his surrogate father. One was about spacing a show, always meticulously planned by Dorsey. The Dorsey band wasn't just playing music for dancers, it was also presenting a show, one that demanded its own structure, intelligent variations of up-tempo tunes and ballads, a sustained presentation that would leave the audience with a sense of completion.

Sinatra told me about Dorsey: "He put together a show like it was one long piece of music, or like an album – this was before the LP, and you couldn't do records that way – with different moods and movements leading to a crescendo. He knew how to shift a mood so it didn't all sound the same and bore the ass off the audience. It was dance music, first and foremost. But it was more than that. I always kept that in mind later, for my own shows and albums. Tommy didn't spell it out to us, but he didn't have to. It became part of you, just from doing it. Seven shows a day, sometimes, if you worked a theater. Three shows a night, if the gig was a dance somewhere. It became part of you."

Dorsey's own work on the trombone had a lasting influence on Sinatra's style. There has been much discussion of the way Sinatra watched Dorsey's tricks of breathing, in order to sustain long phrases. The writer and lyricist Gene Lees dismisses most of that as a myth. But in his essay on Sinatra in *Singers and the Song II*, Lees describes superbly what Dorsey's real influence was on Sinatra the musician. He writes of Dorsey:

"He did ... have remarkable breath control, and his slow deliberate release of air to support long lyrical melodic lines was indeed instructive to Sinatra and still worth any singer's attention. Dorsey would use this control to tie the end of one phrase into the start of the next. Sinatra learned to do the same."

Lees cites, as an example, their 1941 recording of "Without a Song."

"Since Dorsey's trombone solo precedes the vocal, the record provides an opportunity to observe how Sinatra was learning from Dorsey, and how far he had come from 'All or Nothing at All.' At the end of the bridge, Sinatra goes up to a mezzo-forte high note to crest the phrase 'as long as a song is strung in my SOUL!' But he does not breathe then, as most singers would. He drops easily to a soft 'I'll never know ...' This linking of phrases between the inner units, learned from Dorsey, gave Sinatra's work a kind of seamlessness."

To build up his breath, Sinatra spent long hours in swimming pools, often under water, and when not on the road used the outdoor track at a school in Jersey City. Dorsey's long lines, his legato sound, his use of glissando movements, abruptly plunging deep into the lower register for certain effects – all marked Sinatra. But Sinatra could do things Dorsey could not do, for the simple reason that he was using the English language, with its creamy vowels and abrupt consonants. And he used it in a way that can only be described as urban. Again, Lees describes this very well:

"When you sing a long note, it is the vowel you sustain, almost always. Certain of the consonants, voiced or voiceless, cannot be sustained: *b* and its voiceless counterpart *p*, *d* and *t*, *g* and *k*. You cannot sing thattttt. It is impossible. You must sing thaaaaat or cuuuuup. Or taaaaake. But certain other consonants, voiced and unvoiced – *v* and *f*, *z* and *s* – can be sustained, being fricatives, although I find the effect unattractive. You cannot sustain the semivowels *w* and *y*. But there are four semivowels that can be sustained: *m*, *n*, *l*, and *r*. Now, just as Spanish has long and short forms of the letter *r* – a double *rr*, as in *perro*, is rolled – correct Italian enunciation requires that you slightly sustain all double consonants. And Sinatra always recognized this principle, whether because of his Italian background or not. You hear it when he extends the *l* in *Alllll or Nothing at Alllll*."

In addition, Sinatra's delivery of certain words acquired a subtle New York flavor, Lees points out, because he "dentalized" *t*s and *d*s. That is, like many people from the New York area, he formed each consonant with the tongue against the teeth, rather than the gum above the teeth. In words like *dream* or *tree*, he could instantly pull it away, softening the following *r.* This made for a more fluid enunciation of many words and prevented the popping of consonants when using the microphone. This was never a problem for opera singers, or Broadway belters, but was essential when using a microphone in a recording studio, or the even clumsier microphones used on bandstands.

During this period Sinatra worked hard at mastering the microphone, knowing that it was his musical instrument. There were no portable mikes in those days; each microphone was attached to a stand. Almost all singers stood rigidly facing the mike and used their hands for dramatic emphasis. It was as if they were singing to the microphone, not the audience. Sinatra changed that, gripping the stand itself, and then, according to Lees, "moving the mike in accordance with what he was singing. And he was the man who developed this technique." Movement was crucial to the performance. "Sinatra gripped the stand and drew the microphone toward him or tilted it away according to the force of the note he was putting out at any moment."

Sinatra was then able to establish greater intimacy with the audience, shifting his attention from one young fan to another, but making each feel like the specific object of his attention. He never lost that ability to connect. It was at the heart of his intimate style. These factors combined to make the unique Sinatra sound: breath control and seamlessly sustaining notes; the subtlety of the New York speaking voice refined by impeccable diction; a natural, intimate style made possible by intelligent use of the microphone. Dorsey also established for Sinatra a standard of professional excellence that would endure for a lifetime.

Nobody can speak with absolute confidence about the artistic undertones of the Sinatra style. He spoke later in life about the effect of Billie Holiday on his work, citing her phrasing. I've listened to a number of tunes that were recorded by both, and I don't hear that effect. But one night he said something about Lady Day that did make sense.

"What she did was take a song and make it hers," Sinatra said. "She lived inside the song. It didn't matter who wrote the words or the music. She made it hers. All the jerks who fucked her and left her. All the nights strung out on junk. All the crackers that treated her like a nigger. They were all in her music.

That's what she made out of those songs. She made them *her* story."

At his best (and he sometimes made choices that were awful, or had them forced upon him) Sinatra did the same. He inhabited a song the way a great actor inhabits a role, often bringing his own life to the music. As a young singer, there wasn't as much life to draw upon, but it did have a large share of hurts, some because he was Italian American, some because he felt he didn't have enough formal education, others because of the way he grew up as an only child. Right from the beginning, he had a profound understanding of human loneliness. Some of this he must have also drawn from the silent presence of his father, the inconstant exuberance of his mother. Some of it must have been emphasized when he joined the company of the orchestras, living day and night with talented men who had lived other kinds of lives, rich with the presence of family.

"I'd be in the bus, and the guys'd be sleeping or drinking or talking," he said once. "And I'd look out the window and see these houses with the lights on and wonder how they all lived. The houses looked warm. Safe. You know, *normal*. I was still a kid, but I knew that it was too late for me to have that kind of life."

Riding those buses through America, Sinatra also must have known that he could never be a sideman, a part of a group, all for one, one for all. He wasn't raised that way. He was raised to work solo.

III. When the bombs dropped on Pearl Harbor and the Americans finally entered the war, Sinatra was poised to complete a process that had started with Fiorello La Guardia and was solidified by the baseball triumphs of Joe DiMaggio: the integration of the children of Italian immigrants into American life.

A progressive Republican (in opposition to the anti-Italian bosses of Tammany Hall), La Guardia had been elected mayor of New York in 1933 after a splendid career as the first Italian American ever elected to Congress. In some respects, he was not typical of the immigrant experience. He was the son of a Jewish mother from Trieste and a Protestant father who was born in Foggia, in Il Mezzogiorno. Born on Sullivan Street in New York's Little Italy and raised in Arizona where his father served as a U.S. Army bandmaster, Fiorello spoke Italian and Yiddish and had worked as an interpreter at Ellis Island, an experience that made him a lifelong defender of immigrants. He fought for unions. He fought against all forms of racism. He battled anti-Semitism. As a congressman, he had warned the country about the dangers of Prohibition, urging them to reject the Volstead Act. He predicted that it could not be enforced. Nobody listened, but he was right. Fiorello had passion and language and courage. He became the greatest mayor of New York's twentieth century, a star on radio, a national figure. New Yorkers were not alone in thinking about him with affection and respect.

DiMaggio was a year older than Sinatra, the son of immigrants from Isola delle Femmine, a tiny fishing port on the northern coast of Sicily, just west of Palermo. His father arrived at Ellis Island in 1902, the mother the following year, and they soon moved to California, where there was work for an honest fisherman. Joe, the oldest of nine children, arrived at Yankee Stadium for the 1936 season and had a wonderful year for a twenty-one-year-old, batting .323 and hitting 29 home runs. He was shy, even aloof, but had uncommon style, both as a player and as a man. As he matured, he got even better. He hit with power and for average and was a superb outfielder. In 1941 he set a record that has never been broken: he batted safely in 56 consecutive games.

In those years before television, DiMaggio was known all over America. He endorsed products. His face adorned magazine covers. Songs were written about him. That awful phrase "role model" wasn't used in those days; it was enough to be called a hero. DiMaggio was one of them. An American hero. And an Italian American hero too. There were other Italian American baseball players, including Tony Lazzeri before him, and contemporaries such as Frank Crosetti and the shortstop Phil Rizzuto. But DiMaggio was more than a baseball player; he was the epitome of grace. American grace. Italian American grace. Nobody paid much attention to the fact that he kept silent about discrimination against other Americans, including Italian Americans and blacks. That was

Joe. As Gay Talese has observed: "He was and has remained an interior man, ever distant, cautious, never in the forefront with a social conscience. At best, a male Garbo."

To these triumphs of Italian Americans in politics and sports was added another: the sudden arrival of Frank Sinatra as the biggest star in show business. That trio – La Guardia, DiMaggio, and Sinatra – changed forever the way Americans saw Italian Americans. For the first time, Americans with other ethnic origins wanted to be like these children of the Italian migration. And their accomplishments changed the way Italian Americans saw themselves.

The story of Sinatra's explosive arrival as a major American star is, again, a familiar one, a great show business drama played out on the stage of the Paramount Theater in New York. Timing had something to do with it. The war effort was then under way; the Depression was over; and men and women were, suddenly and astonishingly, earning more money in war plants than they had ever imagined possible. (My father went from a $19-a-week job to one that paid $102.) That meant there was a lot more money to spend on entertainment. And as the young men went off to boot camp or basic training, there were a lot more lonely women in the land.

Sinatra and the Dorsey band were in Hollywood, making a small film called *Ship Ahoy*, when the airplanes of the Japanese Imperial Navy ended the Depression by bombing Pearl Harbor. Twice Sinatra tried to enlist in the army, and each time he was turned down because of that punctured eardrum. But he was increasingly anxious to go out on his own, convinced that there would be a huge audience for a new kind of music that went beyond the big band format. It would be built around the singer, as vigorous as swing but made lusher, more romantic with the use of strings. Sinatra didn't want another singer to get there first. Perry Como from the Ted Weems band. Ray Eberle from Glenn Miller. Or even Jack Leonard.

"I didn't want to be left behind," he said later. "I wanted to get there first."

In January 1942, with Dorsey's reluctant permission, the impatient Sinatra cut four sides for the cut-rate Bluebird Records, using Axel Stordahl as the arranger and employing strings and woodwinds for the first time. These were the first records made on his own, without the dominating accompaniment of a star big band. The tunes were "Night and Day," "The Night We Called It a Day," "The Song Is You," and "The Lamplighter's Serenade." The first three would remain part of his repertoire for the rest of his life. He was exultant. Stordahl remembered sitting with Sinatra after the session, listening to acetate disks: "He just couldn't believe his ears. He was so excited."

Those records enhanced his reputation and found their way to another huge emerging market: jukeboxes.

They also increased his obsessive desire to escape from
Dorsey. His 1940 recording with Dorsey of "I'll Never
Smile Again" had spent twelve weeks as the number one
song on the *Billboard* charts, and the same combination
had hits with "Stardust," "Trade Winds," "Our Love
Affair," "This Love of Mine," "Dolores," and "Oh, Look at
Me Now." But those were all perceived as *Tommy
Dorsey* hits, not Frank Sinatra hits. It was the music he
made with Stordahl for Brunswick that came closest to
what Sinatra wanted to do. He also knew that he had a
real opportunity now to fulfill the boast he'd made after
seeing Bing Crosby perform in 1935. That process had already begun. In May 1941 *Billboard* named him the nation's top male vocalist. The same year's *Down Beat* poll
(released in January 1942) also encouraged Sinatra's am-
bition; for the first time since 1937 Bing Crosby had lost
the number one position. The new favorite was Frank
Sinatra. The time to leave was now.

Finally, after giving a year's notice, he broke free
from Tommy Dorsey in the fall of 1942. He further infu-
riated Dorsey by persuading arranger Axel Stordahl to
go with him, at a salary of $650 a week, four times what
Dorsey was paying him. The departure was bitter. Dorsey
was quick to fire people; he could never forgive people
who, in effect, fired him. Before granting him a release,
Dorsey coldly insisted that Sinatra sign a document
awarding Dorsey a third of Sinatra's earnings for the
next ten years, plus an additional 10 percent to Dorsey's

manager. For doing nothing, except letting him go. So much for father figures. By this point, Sinatra was desperate. He signed. He was on his own at last. At first, it wasn't all that easy. Bookers still were more interested in the big swing bands than in solo singers. They didn't fully realize that Sinatra's recordings, played at home, on the radio, or on jukeboxes, were building him a very special audience.

After an impressive engagement at the Mosque Theater in Newark, he was booked into the Paramount as a special added attraction with the Benny Goodman band. This wasn't Goodman's idea; he already featured Peggy Lee as vocalist and Jess Stacy on piano. He and his band were the stars, and Sinatra was only a kind of dessert when Goodman's show was over. But Sinatra wanted desperately to play the Paramount as a solo act, and his instincts were correct. The date was December 30, 1942. He walked out, his suit baggy on his bony frame, more than a little scared, wearing a bow tie that Nancy had made a size larger to hide his Adam's apple. He started singing, *"The bells are ringing, for me and my gal. . . ."* The rest of the words were lost in the screaming.

OH, GOD, FRANK SINATRA COULD BE THE
SWEETEST, MOST CHARMING MAN IN THE WORLD
WHEN HE WAS IN THE MOOD.

—AVA GARDNER

■   ■   ■

I AM VERY MUCH SURPRISED WHAT I HAVE BEEN
READING IN THE NEWSPAPERS BETWEEN YOU
AND YOUR DARLING WIFE. REMEMBER YOU HAVE
A DECENT WIFE AND CHILDREN. YOU SHOULD
BE VERY HAPPY. REGARDS TO ALL.

—TELEGRAM TO FRANK
SINATRA FROM WILLIE
(WILLIE MOORE) MORETTI,
1949

· 5 ·

I'M A FOOL
TO WANT YOU

ONE OF SINATRA'S most mysterious achievements was also the one that allowed him to endure for more than half a century after Harry James heard him in the Rustic Cabin. It was the nature of his audience. Sinatra started out with far more female than male fans. He ended up with more male fans. This happens to very few pop singers.

On the simplest level it was connected to the times themselves. For millions of women during the war, Sinatra was the romantic voice of the American homefront. He was singing to Rosie the Riveter, the symbolic woman who had walked into a war plant and found employment that was ordinarily reserved for men. She was more than a self-reliant patriot or an earner of a day's pay for a day's work. She was something new, and her newness began to transcend the work itself; Rosie the Riveter was soon asserting some of the prerogatives of men — smoking cigarettes, drinking when she wanted to drink, right up against the bar, sleeping around if she wanted to sleep around, or choosing her own erotic fantasies. The music of Frank Sinatra wasn't used only by men to seduce women; during the conflict that Studs Terkel called "the good war," some women used that music, with its expression of sheer *need*, to seduce the available men. Yes, Sinatra was singing to all those girls whose boyfriends were fighting in Anzio or Guadalcanal; some maintained a patriotic virginity; others went their own ways. At the same time, he was singing to those women, of whatever age, who had never managed to find a boyfriend at all and for whom Saturday night truly was the loneliest night of the week.

In his life Sinatra's sudden, immense fame worked as a kind of aphrodisiac. There were then, as there would be during the long reign of rock and roll, groupies who would sleep with famous men to add them to scoreboards; the names were like the downed Messerschmitts or Zeroes painted by pilots on the sides of P-51s during the war. But there were also many less calculating females suddenly knocking on Frank Sinatra's door. He certainly wasn't so perfectly handsome that he seemed unattainable; he looked to some young women that he'd be as happy to meet them as they would be to meet him.

But the Sinatra fantasy was also safe because its consummation seemed so unlikely. The big reason was that he was also married, was living after June 1944 in Toluca Lake, California, with his wife, Nancy, his daughter, Nancy, and after September 28, 1944, his son. The boy was named Franklin (for President Roosevelt) Emanuel (for his agent, Manie Sachs) Sinatra. He wasn't really a "junior" but would be cursed with the label of Frank Jr. for his entire life. In the wartime years Sinatra played by the rules of the publicity game; if that was what was required to become a gigantic star, then that was what he would do. And so he allowed fan magazines to photograph him with his family, first in Hasbrouck Heights, New Jersey (wearing a Crosby-style yacht cap, smoking a *pipe*, posing in the bar of his finished basement), and then in the grander circumstances of Los Angeles. His wife, Nancy, was always there, smiling in an amused way; in public she played the part of the older, wiser woman who was the guarantor of the innocence of the girls who wanted her husband.

This bow to the conventional pieties became part of the double image that Sinatra was conjuring: the traditionalist, with house and family, *and* the potential lover, consumed by loneliness and unrequited love. As a singer, he was almost always the lover. In American music of the time, Bing Crosby was the reigning husband.

He and Crosby met in 1943, liked each other, worked together on radio shows and patriotic rallies. But Crosby successfully presented a reassuring, almost paternal image to the audience, one whose wild oats had long ago been sown, and kept his personal life – and whatever private demons he might have had – safely behind his own walls. With Sinatra, public and private seemed to merge, and the result was a disturbing ambiguity. Yes, he had a wife and children and a house; but in the music he professed a corrosive emptiness, an almost grieving personal unhappiness. The risk attached to his kind of singing was that it promised authenticity of emotion instead of its blithe dismissal or the empty technique of the virtuoso. His singing demanded to be felt, not admired. It always revealed more than it concealed. Unlike the Crosby persona, Sinatra could not laugh off his losses. That transparency was essential to his music. But it didn't make real life easier for him.

While Sinatra's career was taking off after 1943, with hit records, radio shows, and movie contracts, rumors about his private life started finding their way into gossip columns. He was spotted with this starlet or that woman; on the road he seldom slept alone. Or so the rumors said. Some were certainly true. "You're a young guy," he said once, in another context. "You don't say three Hail Marys and pray for sleep." Sex, of course, was also about power. Young women could use sex to impose fleeting power over the famous young man; Sinatra, the new kid in town, could sleep with Hollywood movie stars to prove to himself that he had true power and would never end up back in Hoboken. But he also was learning that even after the most casual feasts, someone presents you with the bill.

Very early he came up against the terrible scrutiny that comes with fame – and he didn't like it at all. It was one thing for an unknown Sinatra to live in Hoboken and have a fling in Englewood; nobody would ever know, except the principals. It was different for a star. Someone was always watching. Years later Sinatra was still struggling with the velvet prison of fame.

"It just changes everything," he said. "You can't go to a beach. You can't walk into a movie. You can't stand on a corner and eat a hot dog. You want the fame but, baby, you pay a price."

During the war, rumors of Sinatra's carousing didn't matter to the young women in the audience. If Sinatra was indeed doing what he was accused of, the female audience wasn't surprised. The subtext of his music suggested that he didn't feel complete in his personal life; in a complicated way, these young fans also wanted the same chance that the other women seemed to be having. Most didn't identify with Nancy; they envied her, even honored her, but they were more like the other women, desiring a night with Frank Sinatra with no illusions about living happily ever after. Everywhere on earth, wartime is a bad time for traditional values. When Sinatra did go home to Nancy, there were often angry confrontations, abrupt denials or dismissals, slammed doors.

Sinatra didn't handle any of this well. It was one thing to create romantic fantasies for strangers; it was quite another to deal directly with a humiliated wife. The emerging truth was quite unremarkable: like many other young men, Frank Sinatra was a good father and a poor husband.

In many ways he was a very lucky American. Timing is everything, in music and life. His career timing had been perfect. He was also lucky to have been declared 4-F. But his good fortune during the war hurt him when it was over. Absorbed with his expanding career, and perhaps fearful of his reception among the GIs, Sinatra didn't make a USO tour until after the war in Europe ended on May 8, 1945. He was accompanied on the six-week tour by comedian Phil Silvers (with whom he had written "Nancy (with the Laughing Face)" as a birthday present for his daughter on her fourth birthday). On the long transatlantic journey to Europe, Sinatra was anxious. There had been predictions that the soldiers might be hostile, might throw eggs or tomatoes at the man who was making their girlfriends and sisters swoon while GIs were fighting the war. That didn't happen. With shrewd advice from Silvers, Sinatra cast himself as a skinny underdog, an ordinary guy much like GI Joe. He made fun of himself and his image. He charmed the grizzled young veterans, expressed his gratitude to them, identified with them, and soon had them identifying with him. The press agents sighed in relief; so did Sinatra. Everything had gone smoothly. He'd even visited Italy and had met the Pope.

But when the veterans started coming home that fall, after the atom bombs ended the war with Japan, the smooth ride of Frank Sinatra started getting bumpier. The return of actors like Clark Gable and Jimmy Stewart reminded Americans that many show business figures had gone off to war. The ballplayers came home too, including Pee Wee Reese and Pete Reiser from the Brooklyn Dodgers, Hank Greenberg from the Detroit Tigers, Ted Williams from the Boston Red Sox, and, of course, the great DiMaggio. All were among the 9 million Americans who had served their country. More than half a million had been Italian Americans, thirteen of whom received the Congressional Medal of Honor while ten were awarded the Navy Cross. More than 300,000 Americans didn't come home at all, including 13,712 from the state of New Jersey. And in every state in the Union, those who had been wounded and maimed tried to adjust to the changed country. Some have speculated about the effect military service might have had on Sinatra's personality and career; that leads nowhere. For reasons that were honorable, he didn't go to his generation's war and had to settle for playing servicemen in eleven of his sixty movies. One thing is certain: for many of those who came back from World War II, the music of Frank Sinatra was no consolation for their losses. Some had lost friends. Some had lost wives and lovers. All had lost portions of their youth.

More important to the Sinatra career, the girls from the Paramount, and all their sisters around the country, started marrying the men who came home. Bobby socks vanished from many closets. The girls who once wore them had no need anymore for imaginary lovers; they had husbands. Nothing is more embarrassing to grownups than the passions of adolescence, and for many, Frank Sinatra was *the* teenage passion. Children were soon being born in unprecedented numbers, all those kids who a generation later would be known as the baby boomers. At the same time, the children of all those turn-of-the-century immigrants, now toughened by war, equipped with the benefits of the GI Bill, began leaving city ghettos for the expanding new suburbs; some became the first people in the histories of their families to go to universities.

Swing music was rapidly dying, for complicated reasons. Most important was a two-year strike by the American Federation of Musicians, which, among other things, forced Sinatra to make his first sides for Columbia Records singing a cappella with a choral group. The strike kept the big bands out of the studios, unable to reach the mass audience with new material. Goodman, Dorsey, and others sounded stale; Glenn Miller was dead, having disappeared over the English Channel. The economics of the bands also changed. Postwar inflation drove up the cost of transportation. Sidemen who gladly worked for $40 a week during the Depression were now asking for $200, with soloists demanding more. Musically, the big band sound was exhausted. From Fifty-second Street to Minton's Playhouse in Harlem, the hippest fans were now listening to bebop, to Charlie Parker and Dizzy Gillespie, Fats Navarro, Max Roach, and others – all of them playing in small groups that were formed during the musicians' strike. Jazz had become a freer, more democratic form of chamber music, an ongoing jam session liberated from the dictates of rigid big band arrangements. Younger fans, with only vague memories of the Depression, were listening to mush or to novelty tunes. For many other people, the music of the swing bands reminded them of the war, a time they wanted to forget. It would be a long time before nostalgia would work its magic, transforming that music into a symbol of a more innocent America.

Musically, Sinatra reacted to the postwar climate in several ways. Even before leaving for his USO tour, he had experimented with other sounds, recording four sides with a black gospel-style group called the Charioteers and two others in a rumba rhythm with the orchestra of Xavier Cugat. He conducted an instrumental album of Alec Wilder songs. He wrote the lyrics to an aching ballad called "This Love of Mine." But basically, he stayed with variations on his own traditional taste in ballads and jump tunes, most of them arranged by Stordahl. Many were very well done, enriched by strings and woodwinds, but the mysterious currents of public taste were shifting. The fans were groping for something new, sounds that would express the exuberance, optimism, and, in certain ways, mindlessness of the years after the war. Some would find it in singers as varied as Billy Eckstine, Frankie Laine, and Guy Mitchell. Perry Como had a string of hits. Doris Day became a star, along with Peggy Lee, Vaughn Monroe, Vic Damone, and the Four Aces. Even Gene Autry had a hit in 1949 with "Rudolph the Red Nosed Reindeer." There were no signs of panic in Frank Sinatra, but he must have been uneasy.

He put much of his energy into the movies. In 1945 he won a special Academy Award for a ten-minute short called *The House I Live In*. He played himself, leaving a radio studio and running into some kids who are beating up another "because we don't like his religion." Sinatra tries to straighten them out and sings the title song. At the time, Sinatra's liberal politics were widely known. Most performers of that era kept their politics to themselves; let Democrats in the audience believe they were Democrats, Republicans think they were Republicans. But Sinatra was a new breed in Hollywood. He publicly supported Franklin D. Roosevelt and visited him in the White House. This was more than familial loyalty to his mother, Dolly; Sinatra was one of the first big stars to use his fame to promote his politics, and those politics were, by all accounts, deeply felt. He made an effort to visit schools and talk to teenagers about bigotry, always citing the hurtful words that had been hurled at him as a boy in Hoboken. He signed petitions. He sent money to candidates. The short, directed by Mervyn LeRoy from a script by Albert Maltz (later to become one of the Hollywood Ten during the anticommunist crusade), impressed the critics.

"Mr. Sinatra takes his popularity seriously," said the reviewer for *Cue*. "More, he attempts to do something constructive with it. Millions, young and old, who will not or cannot read between the lines of their daily newspapers and are blind to the weed-like growth of bigotry and intolerance planted by hate-ridden fanatics, will listen carefully to what Mr. Sinatra has to say in this short film."

He followed the short with *Anchors Aweigh* (1945), a bright, good-natured musical about sailors on shore leave. Sinatra was superb. He worked with Gene Kelly — worked very hard indeed, and his dance number with Kelly shows it; the routine is full of high spirits, self-kidding, and good dancing. "I never worked so goddamned hard in my life," he said later, laughing in a fond way. "Kelly was a brute." But those were the days of the major studios; at MGM, where Sinatra had a five-year contract, he often couldn't choose his vehicles. The films that followed were mediocre (*It Happened in Brooklyn*, RKO's *The Miracle of the Bells*), and one, *The Kissing Bandit*

(1948), was dreadful. Set in the nineteenth century, this semimusical stars Sinatra as a young Mexican fresh out of an Eastern college who goes back to Old California to run the family rancho. He even sings one song while riding a white horse. Sinatra's love interest is Kathryn Grayson, and the movie also features J. Carrol Naish, the Irish actor from *Life with Luigi*, who plays Sinatra's Mexican foreman, Chico. "I hated reading the script," Sinatra later said, "hated doing it, and, most of all, hated seeing it. So did everyone else."

He wasn't truly good again as a movie actor until 1949, when he teamed up once more with Kelly in an MGM musical called *Take Me Out to the Ball Game*, and quickly followed it with a movie masterpiece, *On the Town*. Another story of sailors on shore leave, this time in New York, the film was codirected by Kelly (who also stars) and Stanley Donen. It was written by Betty Comden and Adolph Green. Music for a ballet was composed by Leonard Bernstein. The reviews were raves. Sinatra's star should have been ascending.

Instead, he was heading for the Fall.

II. The Fall was essential to the Sinatra myth. Most of it was a combination of bad timing, dreadful luck, and self-inflicted wounds. It didn't happen all at once; instead, the Fall started small and gathered strength, like a landslide.

First, Sinatra alienated the Hollywood press corps. He would have one too many drinks in some public place

and curse them all for whores and pimps. He started
firing off thin-skinned telegrams to various columnists,
including Louella Parsons, then the most famous paid
yenta in Hollywood. In 1946 the Hollywood Women's
Press Club gave Sinatra the "Least Cooperative Actor"
award. He was not contrite. Then, on April 8, 1947, in
Ciro's nightclub in Hollywood, Sinatra punched out
Hearst columnist Lee Mortimer, who had been needling
him in print for many months. The cops were called.
Charges were filed. Sinatra was arrested. To be sure, it
was not as if he had punched out Mother Cabrini. In almost four decades in the newspaper business, I have
never met anybody who liked or respected Lee Mortimer; he was a nasty, mean man, a poor reporter, a
worse writer, and the king of the "blind item." But it was
a critical mistake for Sinatra to belt him. Newspaper
people who despised Mortimer suddenly started getting
much tougher about Frank Sinatra; as contemptible as
Mortimer was, he was part of their guild, not Sinatra's.
The singer had to pay Mortimer $9,000 to settle out of
court. But there were more lasting consequences. The
Hearst chain was then a powerful national force and had
already been sniping at Sinatra over his liberal politics.
Now the attacks intensified. He was Red-baited by the
chain's star columnists, Westbrook Pegler and George
Sokolsky, and subjected to a campaign that dripped with
innuendo. Sinatra was presented as naive or gullible at
best, an agent of the Red conspiracy at worst. Sinatra, of

course, wasn't close to being a communist; he was, like millions of other Americans, a committed New Deal liberal. But the Hearstlings didn't care about the facts. They wanted to destroy Sinatra, and in the growing postwar anticommunist hysteria, they had many allies. Hollywood was becoming a major target of the anticommunist crusaders; the cynical among them knew that hauling a Hollywood figure before a committee would bring bigger headlines than would interrogating some high school math teacher who had been a communist for three weeks in 1934. The true believers among the crusaders were convinced that Moscow was smuggling anti-American propaganda into the most brainless Hollywood productions. Most of this was absurd. But studio bosses were never profiles in courage, and because of their fear and trembling, the blacklist soon became a fact of Hollywood life. Sinatra was marginal to that story but never completely immune. In the placid postwar years he was starting to look like a whole lot of trouble.

Early in 1947 Sinatra did another job on himself, providing a context for the Mortimer affair and building a crucial element in his life that would stay around until he died. At some point in January he accepted an invitation to go to Havana from Joe Fischetti, the youngest of the three Fischetti brothers, who were among the second-generation hoodlums then running the Chicago rackets established during Prohibition by Al Capone. Sinatra had known the Fischetti brothers from before the war, when he had played a joint they ran in Chicago. Sinatra said, Why not? In those days a trip to Havana was as routine as one to Miami.

But there are several ways to interpret this journey. One is dark. According to this version, Frank Sinatra had been connected to the Mob for at least five years. In particular, he was obligated to them for one big favor. Back in 1943, when he was at the peak of the first stage of his fame, he was also being ruined financially by the terms of the release he had signed with Tommy Dorsey. The bandleader insisted on taking almost 55 percent of Sinatra's earnings; expenses and taxes consumed the rest. Dorsey refused to negotiate; a deal was a deal, and fuck you, kid. So Sinatra reached out to the Mob. In some versions of the tale, Dolly Sinatra went personally to see Longie Zwillman at his mansion in New Jersey; in others, Sinatra made the visit himself. Zwillman was outraged at the injustice of it all and put Willie Moretti on the case. In the spirit of conciliation and compromise, Moretti walked into Dorsey's dressing room, shoved a pistol into the bandleader's mouth, and told him to give Frank Sinatra a release. Dorsey instantly agreed.

Most Sinatra biographers, including those who are not soft on Sinatra's personal history, dismiss this story as pure invention. The research indicates that Sinatra obtained his release after a year of tough bargaining by his powerful agents from the Music Corporation of America (MCA) and some equally tough lawyers. Dorsey was persuaded that he could not afford the publicity that would come his way if the contract became the center of a court case; Sinatra, after all, was among the most popular entertainers in the United States. Dorsey settled for $60,000, and he and Sinatra went their separate, if unhappy ways. The myth has a certain logic and great durability. I heard it as a teenager from the apprentice hoodlums I knew in Brooklyn; it was repeated to me by cops and old reporters when I was a young newspaperman.

For whatever reason, in February 1947 Sinatra flew to Havana, promising to meet Nancy later in Mexico City. Alas, he was photographed getting off a plane with Joe Fischetti. Both men were wearing sunglasses and carrying attaché cases; they definitely looked like a pair of gangsters. They went to the Hotel Nacional, then the grandest hotel in the Cuban capital, and checked into separate rooms. Sinatra immediately found himself at the largest Mob convention since the late 1920s. The most honored guest was Charles (Lucky) Luciano himself.

It remains unclear whether Sinatra knew that Luciano would be in Havana; if he did, it should be no surprise that he would want to meet him. Charlie Lucky was a legendary figure during Sinatra's youth and was still one of the most famous gangsters in the world. The romantic aura of the bootlegger was still attached to such men; they were not yet committed to the wholesale peddling of heroin. Luciano was then living in exile in

Naples as the result of a deal worked out during the war whereby the imprisoned Mob boss agreed to do what he could to help the war effort. Or so we were told by purveyors of the myth. Luciano bragged later that he had made this deal while serving a thirty-to-fifty-year sentence for white slavery in Dannemora prison. (That sentence, by the way, was almost certainly the result of a frame-up.) Luciano claimed that he had helped secure the New York waterfront against sabotage and then set up intelligence networks for the Allies before the invasion of Sicily. The grateful Americans then cut his sentence, released him in 1946, and deported him to Naples. He couldn't return to the United States but was, of course, free to go to Cuba. The Mob bosses – including Frank Costello, Meyer Lansky, Carlos Marcello, Joe Adonis, and dozens of others – had assembled to honor Charlie Lucky, pledge loyalty, deliver him some cash, discuss business (including a plan to kill Bugsy Siegel, who was not in Havana but preparing to invent modern Las Vegas). They would also have fun.

Luciano claimed later, in a posthumous "autobiography," that one of the purposes of the Havana assembly was to congratulate young Frank Sinatra for his great accomplishments and to allow Sinatra to thank them for all their help. This seems preposterous; why risk calling attention to their own clandestine congress by bringing a man so famous to a public place? It's more likely that young Fischetti was running his own game: trying to impress his elders by producing Frank Sinatra and to impress Sinatra by displaying his own intimate connections to some legendary mobsters. Fischetti seems to have introduced Sinatra to all of them. There was one report that Sinatra got up to sing in the nightclub of the Hotel Nacional. A few days later he left to meet his wife on St. Valentine's Day in Mexico City.

That should have been that; as Sinatra was learning, that is almost never that. Scripps Howard columnist Robert Ruark, who was in Havana, learned about Luciano's presence from Narcotics Bureau boss Harry J. Anslinger, a bumbling fanatic who was engaged in a turf war with J. Edgar Hoover of the FBI. Anslinger (or one of his agents) underlined Sinatra's part in the "convention." Ruark, a macho right-winger who despised Sinatra's politics, opened up with all his rhetorical guns. He wrote a column that said, in part:

"Mr. Sinatra, the self-confessed savior of the country's small fry, by virtue of his lectures on clean living and love-thy-neighbor, his movie shorts on tolerance, and his frequent dabblings into the do-good department of politics, seems to be setting a most peculiar example for his hordes of pimply, shrieking slaves, who are alleged to regard him with the same awe as a practicing Mohammedan for the Prophet."

There was an immense scandal. Lucky Luciano! Frank Sinatra! The sin city of Havana! It was a splendid opportunity to attack Sinatra's politics as more than

naive, as probably devious. All the old anti-Italian preju-
dices rose again, clothed, as always, in virtue. Sinatra
said, "I was brought up to shake a man's hand when I am
introduced to him without first investigating his past."
But the damage was done. The Mob image would be part
of the rest of his life. Thirty years later he admitted to me
about the Havana trip: "It was one of the dumbest things
I ever did." But he did not elaborate.

There would be other Mob stories over the years: his
long friendship with Sam (Momo) Giancana of Chicago,
his ease with West Coast hoodlum Mickey Cohen, his
connections with some members of the Patriarca family
of Rhode Island. He certainly played Las Vegas in the
heyday of the hoodlums and helped make it one of the
nation's most lucrative adult playgrounds. He played
Mob joints in other parts of the country, sometimes without a fee. At every Sinatra concert I attended over the
years, I would see known wise guys, smoking cigars, their
diamond pinkie rings glittering in the light. At concerts
in New York they brought their wives; in Vegas they
brought their girlfriends. As late as 1976 Sinatra posed
for a photograph in his dressing room at the Westchester
Premier Theater with Brooklyn Mob boss Carlo Gambino and a group of other hoodlums. It didn't matter that
they wanted the photograph to impress their friends and
children, it didn't matter that they were among Sinatra's
most awestruck fans; they had access.

It's absurd to believe that the Mob had made Sinatra

a star; if that was possible, they'd have made two hundred other stars, and they made absolutely none. But Sinatra certainly knew Mob guys, was often amused by them, and knew that they could be dangerous. When we were talking about doing his book in the mid-1970s, I told him I'd have to discuss three subjects with him: his politics, his women, and the Mob. He shrugged and said that the first two were no problem. "But if I talk about those other guys, someone might come knocking at my fucking door." A few days later he called and said, "Hey, what the hell. All the guys I knew are dead anyway." On another occasion he elaborated about his friendships with hoodlums:

"Did I know those guys? Sure, I knew some of those guys. I spent a lot of time working in saloons. And saloons are not run by the Christian Brothers. There were a lot of guys around, and they came out of Prohibition, and they ran pretty good saloons. I was a kid. I worked in the places that were open. They paid you, and the checks didn't bounce. I didn't meet any Nobel Prize winners in saloons. But if Francis of Assisi was a singer and worked in saloons, he would've met the same guys. That doesn't make him part of something. They said hello, you said hello. They came backstage. They thanked you. You offered them a drink. That was it." He paused. "And it doesn't matter anymore, does it? Most of the guys I knew, or met, are dead."

But in 1948-49, as he moved inexorably toward the

Fall, the Mob was becoming a heavier piece of his baggage. There were more severe, if less melodramatic, problems. His marriage was in constant turmoil; Nancy was holding on, hoping to wait him out as he dallied elsewhere; Sinatra wanted his total freedom. The move to California had put a continent between him and his parents, but the city of New York would serve Sinatra for another half-century as his personal version of the Old Country. It would always be as full of magic as it had been when he stood alone on the piers of Hoboken. If he felt the urge, he wanted the freedom to go back – alone. To move through the New York night. Without a wife. Without his children. The marriage was Hoboken, and Hoboken was not magic.

Later, most people who were sympathetic to both parties said that Sinatra had grown and Nancy had not, that he was out in the big world, adding sophistication and social ease to his style, while Nancy remained imprisoned by the parochial codes of New Jersey. Sinatra once told a close friend about the night he realized the marriage was over. He had to go to a business meeting in a Los Angeles restaurant. It was raining hard. When he reached the door, Nancy called after him, "Frank, don't forget your galoshes."

That story might be apocryphal; it too neatly fits the story of Sinatra's flight from the middle-class values of Hoboken. But many of the others were not. There were constant arguments over money, houses, the children, relatives, other women. He and Nancy separated at least once, in 1948, but reconciled after a few weeks. With very little discretion, Sinatra romanced a variety of women, including Marilyn Maxwell and Lana Turner; and then in 1949 he met Ava Gardner.

III. The tale of Frank Sinatra and Ava Gardner has been told many times, most effectively and honestly by Ava herself in her autobiography *(Ava)*. At one point, the whole world seemed to know the story of the romance, Sinatra's divorce, the marriage to Ava, the mutual jealousies, the drunken quarrels, the snarling fights with photographers and reporters. At one point, Sinatra even tried to kill himself. In the sorry narrative that constitutes the Fall, he would lose his movie contract, his radio show, his recording contract, and his agents. Desperate for money as the various contracts began running out, needing the validation of an audience, he began taking as many live engagements as possible. And then he lost his voice. That was the most terrifying event of all. It happened in the spring of 1950, near the end of an eight-week engagement at the Copacabana nightclub in New York, and he described the night to Arlene Francis many years later:

"I was doing three shows a night, five radio shows a week, benefit performances, and recording at the same time. And then I opened at the Capitol Theater toward the end of the engagement. I went out to do the third show [at the Copa] at about half past two or quarter to three in the morning, and I went for a note, and nothing came out. Not a sound came out. And I merely said to the audience, as best I could, 'Good night.'"

Sinatra would get his voice back and continue to work; in that same year of 1950 he still had several years left on his Columbia Records contract. But as a singer he was confused, often torn, capable of fine work on "Hello, Young Lovers," "Birth of the Blues," and "Why Try to Change Me Now?" while recording such second-rate tunes as "Tennessee Newsboy" and the infamous "Mama Will Bark," a duet with a bosomy TV star named Dagmar. The hit-driven Mitch Miller, boss of Columbia Records, was often blamed for the erratic quality of Sinatra's work. But he insisted later that Sinatra could never be forced to make any record and that he had agreed to even the Dagmar duet. Certainly, Sinatra was desperate for a hit. He hated the new music, songs like Frankie Laine's "Mule Train" or "Come On-a My House," performed by Rosemary Clooney (a singer he otherwise admired); but while his singles were selling 25,000 copies, others' were soaring over a million, and Mitch Miller had produced them.

At the heart of Sinatra's anxiety was his fading relationship with the audience. Men had never been a major part of that audience; the outbreak of the Korean War in June 1950 reminded many of them that Sinatra had never taken part in World War II. Some veterans of that war (including baseball great Ted Williams) were now being called back to active duty while Sinatra had never served a day (neither had John Wayne, but right-wing actors were never criticized in the way that liberal actors were attacked). The Cold War was now hot; communist troops were killing America's young men in the Korean peninsula. The great hunt for domestic subversives, for pinkos, com-symps, the enemy within, became even more intense. Joe McCarthy, the junior senator from Wisconsin, emerged as the major voice sniffing into past associations with communists, suggesting evidence of wide conspiracies, and he was not alone. From California the crusade was driven by an ambitious young politician named Richard Nixon. Liberalism itself was soon reeling, with some Republicans describing the long reign of Roosevelt and his successor, Harry Truman, as "twenty years of treason." It did not help Sinatra's reputation that he had supported Henry Wallace for president in 1948.

In 1950 another kind of inquiry into domestic enemies began. The Kefauver hearings into organized crime became a television extravaganza, helping to establish the new medium. Elaborate organizational charts were presented, showing the way territory was divvied up by the Mob. The word *Mafia* was shouted from headlines. Connections between Mob guys and big-city political machines were explored. Among many others, the names of Longie Zwillman and Willie Moretti were tossed around, the refrain of "I refuse to answer on grounds that I will tend to incriminate myself" was heard in the land, and there were more rehashed stories about the famous summit conference in Havana. Mobology became a staple of the newspapers, and many reprinted the photograph of Sinatra and Joe Fischetti getting off that plane. Some of the more creative journalists even claimed to know that each attaché case contained a million dollars, in spite of that being a physical impossibility.

If Sinatra's triumphs were, in part, a result of the times of World War II, his defeats would be part of the times of the early 1950s. His politics were suddenly a bit musty to some, un-American to others; as the exodus of blacks from the South got under way, the contempt for liberalism also acquired an element of racism. Sinatra's urban, freewheeling style, with its reminders of immigrant origins, was suspect in white Middle America and its expanding suburbs, where the demand for conformity was growing more powerful. His connections to the Mob, real or illusory, outraged more and more city people as the heroin plague spread and the crime rate soared. The bootlegger might have been a romantic figure; there was nothing romantic about a dope peddler. In some ways, Sinatra was a public figure who fed two paranoid visions: the secret society of the Mob and the agenda of the liberal left. On the crudest level, this did not help him sell records. It certainly did not help him sell records to men. Older men sneered at Sinatra. Younger men were listening to Frankie Laine and Guy Mitchell.

Much more dangerous to Sinatra was his abandonment by female fans. This almost certainly was the result of his brutal public humiliation of his wife. It was one thing to have discreet affairs, but flaunting Ava Gardner during a January 1950 gig at the Shamrock Hotel in Houston, *while still married to Nancy* – that was cruel. His third child, daughter Tina, was only a year and a half old. The boy, Frank Jr., was five. But little Nancy was eight. She was going to school. She could hear the taunts. Her mother, a beautiful, normal woman, was being tossed aside for an actress who was once married to *Mickey Rooney!* This was outrageous. Or so believed many of the women who in 1944 and 1945 had bought millions of Sinatra's records or had waited in the rain to see him at the Paramount. So they left. Many never came back. They identified too strongly with Nancy Barbato Sinatra, who soon settled into the role she would play for the rest of Sinatra's life: the Woman Who Would Wait. Asked once why she had never remarried, she answered, "After *Sinatra?*"

The loss of that core audience was a source of pervasive, contaminating anguish for Sinatra. He was only ten years removed from the Rustic Cabin; now his nights were haunted by the dread of losing everything, of a forced return to the maiming obscurity of his youth.

More than many other performers, he needed the audience. He needed to feel a connection with all those strangers, needed them to ratify his existence and his value, needed to feed on their emotions, as they sometimes were nourished by his. And now they were gone. Or so it seemed. And without the audience, he was just the boy who was applauded for knowing the words. Or worse: an older man singing to an empty room.

It was the aftermath of the Fall that changed the audience and changed Sinatra. Right out there in public, Sinatra had been flattened. And men often saw the world in sports terms. One thing they knew about prizefighters, for example, was that you never knew what a fighter was made of until he had been knocked down. Second-raters stayed down and took the count. The great ones always got up.

Sinatra got up.

THE HEAD HE
TURNED TOWARD ME WORE A
FACE LIKE MINE.

—W. S. MERWIN

· 6 ·

ALL OF ME

AFTER THE FALL, the Comeback.

For two long and terrible years, Sinatra was a mess. He continued working, making records, appearing on television, performing in small clubs. But in 1952 and 1953 he had no records at all on the *Billboard* singles charts; he had made those lists every previous year since 1940. His three-year television contract with CBS was canceled after thirteen weeks because he wouldn't take the time to rehearse and was abusive to too many people. A 1952 movie called *Meet Danny Wilson* contained many semi-autobiographical touches, including a racketeer who takes 50 percent of the earnings of a singer played by Sinatra. The movie has many fine songs, including "All of Me," "I've Got a Crush on You," "That Old Black

Magic," and "She's Funny That Way." But it was poorly directed and shabbily produced. Sinatra did a live engagement to help the movie when it opened at the Paramount in New York in 1952. That year I was sixteen, and I went to see him, for the first time, in the theater that only eight years earlier was loud with hysterical adoration. He was as good as everybody said he was: in command, singing with energy and feeling. But the theater was half empty. In other parts of the United States the movie opened and closed. That seemed to be the end of Frank Sinatra's Hollywood career.

Sinatra was drinking hard and smoking too much, and then drinking again. Failure stoked the fires of his rage and increased his need for alcohol; both increased his sense of personal dissolution. His artistic energies were also being exhausted by the fierce entanglement with Ava Gardner. Any love affair is a creative act, part imagination, part practice; often, it can lift an artist to new levels of exalted energy. But a doomed and tumultuous love affair, on the model of the Sinatra and Gardner coupling, can destroy creativity. For months their affair and marriage seemed to obliterate the basic optimism required by the romantic impulse, so essential to Sinatra's art. The vision of earthly happiness, that elusive goal that calls forth so much lyricism, was being maimed by a corrosive cynicism.

While Sinatra's career declined, Ava's star shone more brightly. He began to resemble an adjunct to her career, following her to movie locations in Spain, England, Africa, and Mexico. They drank hard. They quarreled. They reconciled. Sometimes Sinatra did his drinking in the empty time when she was away making movies and he was trying to make an impact on television. But distance didn't help him regain clarity or a sense of perspective. Instead, jealousy ate at his guts. In Clarke's or Toots Shor's in New York, in the haunts of a fading Hollywood, or in his own apartment (since he and Ava never did establish a home), he seemed to bounce off the walls, like a drunk who had stayed too long at a party.

But then, slowly, there was a shift. He tried, and failed, to get the part of Johnny Romano in the film of Willard Motley's *Knock on Any Door*; the role went to young John Derek, whose impossibly perfect looks resembled an illustration from *Cosmopolitan* magazine. Sinatra, at thirty-four, was too old, but Johnny Romano's motto was one that Sinatra might have felt deeply: "Live fast, die young, and have a good-looking corpse."

After he was dropped by MCA, Sinatra moved to the William Morris agency and began focusing his attention on a novel by James Jones called *From Here to Eternity*. The book was a huge bestseller, a densely detailed story about soldiers based in Schofield Barracks in Pearl Harbor on the eve of the Japanese attack. All the characters, in one form or another, had been shaped by Prohibition and the Depression, but Sinatra focused on the role of a tough little Italian American named Angelo Maggio. "I knew Maggio," Sinatra said. "I grew up with him in Hoboken." Unlike *Meet Danny Wilson,* this was to be a major film, with a healthy budget; it would have what Sinatra liked to call "class." It was to be made by Columbia Pictures, whose boss was the tough, vulgar Harry Cohn. The director was to be Fred Zinnemann. His *High Noon* the year before was a parable about McCarthyism that simultaneously breathed new life into the western and into the career of Gary Cooper, who won an Academy Award as best actor. Sinatra began to plead for a chance to play Maggio.

He had a little help from his friends. There is neither proof nor logic to Mario Puzo's fictional version in *The Godfather,* where the Mob cuts off the head of a racehorse owned by the studio boss and deposits it in his bed, thus persuading the studio to give the part to a character based loosely on Sinatra. To be sure, Cohn knew Longie Zwillman, who had an affair with Columbia star Jean Harlow in the 1930s, and probably took loans from Zwillman in the lean days of the Depression. But Maggio was a minor part in a movie starring Burt Lancaster, Montgomery Clift, and Deborah Kerr. If the Mob had occult powers, why not get him the starring role? The myth endures. As Mario Puzo himself once said, fiction is the art of "retrospective falsification."

The facts were more banal. Sinatra's new agents were working hard behind the scenes. Sinatra himself pleaded with producer Buddy Adler for a chance to do a screen test. He also called Adler's boss, Harry Cohn, who owed him a favor. More important, Ava interceded with Cohn's wife, Joan, who put in a good word with her husband. Ava also met with Cohn himself, offering to make a movie at Columbia for nothing, if only he'd give Sinatra the part of Maggio. The studio moved cautiously, primarily because the success of *High Noon* had given director Zinnemann some power; they could suggest Sinatra but couldn't order him into the movie. Most of the key players at the studio, including Zinnemann, believed that Sinatra was primarily a singer, not an actor, and would add nothing to the movie's box-office appeal. Everybody in Hollywood knew that Sinatra was a troubled man, increasingly viewed by the public as Mr. Ava Gardner. It would be better to just get a good actor. A fine, but then unknown, New York actor named Eli Wallach was the favorite.

In November 1952 Sinatra was in Kenya with Ava as she worked with Clark Gable and Grace Kelly in John Ford's *Mogambo*. At this point, he seemed to have given up any realistic hope of getting the part. Then, suddenly, the call came from Columbia, asking him to fly home for a screen test. Sinatra was elated. So was Ava. Sinatra took the next plane out. Without Frank's knowledge, Ava flew to London for her second abortion of the year.

Sinatra's screen test was splendid. When it was over, Zinnemann called Adler and said, "You'd better come down here. You'll see something unbelievable." At the same time, Sinatra's luck began to return. The men who made such decisions agreed that Wallach's screen test was even better than Sinatra's. But then Wallach got the opportunity to work with director Elia Kazan on *Camino Real*, the new play by Tennessee Williams. Kazan and Williams were at the peak of their artistic success; Wallach chose the theater over the movies. And Sinatra agreed to play Maggio for a mere $8,000. Shooting would begin in March of 1953. Nobody yet knew it, not even Sinatra, but the Comeback had begun.

III. Musically, Sinatra was also getting up off the floor. In March 1952, in a studio in New York, he made one of his last great records for Columbia, a song called "I'm a Fool to Want You." For many people, including Sinatra, as I saw almost twenty years later in P. J. Clarke's, it became the abridged version of his relationship with Ava. He is supposed to have done it in one take, before walking out into the night alone. He had again merged his life with his art. But the song did not sell; it was, in fact, released as the flip side of the infamous single with Dagmar. By the end of the year he knew that his career at Columbia Records was over, that his contract would not be renewed. On September 17, 1952, he made an elegant recording of Cy Coleman's "Why Try to Change Me Now?" And that tortured part of his professional life was over.

The musical part of the Comeback took place at Capitol Records. The only major record company then based in Los Angeles, it was producing many hits for Nat Cole, Kay Starr, and the team of Les Paul and Mary Ford. Among its founders were songwriters Johnny Mercer and Buddy DeSylva. They respected the music of the big bands and recorded Stan Kenton and Woody Herman, along with older stars such as Benny Goodman, Charlie Barnet, and Duke Ellington. They obviously believed that instant hits were not the only music that could make money; in the long run, excellence would pay off too. The technology of the Capitol studios was top of the line. Sinatra was at such a low point in his career (and facing serious doubts among some Capitol executives) that he was given only a one-year contract, with options for another six, and had to pay for his own recording sessions. Still, after the long misery at Columbia, he once more had a musical home.

At first, he did more of what he had been doing. His first Capitol recording session took place on April 2, 1953, after his return from eight exhilarating weeks of work on *From Here to Eternity*. Once again, he used Axel Stordahl as his arranger and recorded "Lean Baby" (words set to a riff-driven Billy May instrumental), "Don't Make a Beggar Out of Me," "Day In, Day Out," and "I'm Walking Behind You" (which would be a huge hit for Eddie Fisher). There was a renewed confidence in Sinatra's voice, as if he knew just how good he had been in the movie and was anticipating what was coming. But he was not yet the great Sinatra; there was a feeling in the songs that we had been there before. They were released as singles and did not sell. Then there was another moment of good luck. Stordahl was signed as musical director of Eddie Fisher's new television show. Sinatra had two more studio sessions scheduled before leaving on a long summer tour of Europe. He needed a new arranger in a hurry.

Alan Livingston, then a vice-president in charge of artists and repertoire at Capitol Records, had already brought up a name.

"Do me one favor, and do yourself a favor," Livingston told Sinatra. "Work with Nelson Riddle."

And so he did.

III. Nelson Smock Riddle Jr. was born in Hackensack, New Jersey, on June 1, 1921, about a half an hour from where Frank Sinatra was growing up in a much different way. Riddle's father, of Anglo-Irish and Dutch descent, was a commercial artist who loved popular music and played a little trombone. His mother had Alsatian and Spanish roots and loved the literary and musical classics. Both parents encouraged their son's musical ambitions. Riddle started taking piano lessons when he was eight, and when he was fourteen, he turned to the trombone, using his father's instrument. That was 1935, and again we see the effects of the Depression. He began taking trombone lessons from a Professor Dittamo in Paterson.

"After eight lessons," Riddle wrote, in an autobio-
graphical sketch published in 1985, "the professor told
me not to come again, since my dad had not paid him
anything so far. It seems his fee was one dollar a lesson,
and this being 1935, *dimes*, much less *dollars*, were difficult to come by for anything more esoteric than a loaf of
bread."

The piano lessons stopped; the music didn't. Riddle
joined the Ridgewood High School band and, after his
junior year, started playing with "kid bands" around the
town of Rumson, getting permission from his parents to
stay alone in a summer bungalow without electricity.
Just before his senior year, he met Bill Finegan, who was
older than Riddle and already arranging for bands out of
his home in Rumson. "We would sit up all night listening
to classical music, especially that of Shostakovich, whose
First Symphony, premiered in 1937, captured Bill's interest and imagination." Finegan began teaching Riddle the
basics of arranging for dance bands, giving him assign-
ments, correcting his work. Those lessons ended when
Finegan went off to work for Glenn Miller. But he had set
some high standards for young Riddle.

"Bill Finegan taught me to enjoy and appreciate the
classics as the prime source of musical richness," Riddle
remembered later. "He also, by example, showed me that
much effort is required to produce one's best work and
that it is unwise and unfair to settle for any less. I remember showing up for a lesson one afternoon and be-

ing confronted by a very exhausted Finegan, up all the previous night, unshaven, red-eyed, and standing in the midst of a small pile of score pages, representing no less than *twenty-six* possible introductions for the same arrangement, as yet unfinished."

During this period one of Riddle's aunts gave him one of those wind-up Victrolas that were changing Frank Sinatra's Hoboken, along with the rest of the country. She also presented him with a 78 rpm recording of Debussy performed by Paderewski. He remembered playing it over and over again, trying to understand its components. In the bungalow in Rumson, however, he had no radio. On weekends Riddle's father would drive down from his studio in Ridgewood, and the young musician would sit in his father's car, listening to classical and popular music on the car radio. Often the car battery would go dead. "In contrast, however, my personal musical battery was always 'super-charged' by the time the weekend was over."

On his nineteenth birthday, in 1940, Riddle landed his first professional job, playing trombone and doing some minor arranging for an Artie Shaw carbon copy named Tommy Reynolds, and then moved up to the Charlie Spivak orchestra. This was a good swing band, ranking just below the top level, and it was a great place to serve an apprenticeship. Riddle spent two years with Spivak, learning something every day, as Sinatra had with Harry James and Tommy Dorsey. But now the war was on, and Riddle was facing the draft. To avoid the army, he left Spivak for the Merchant Marine band, based in Sheepshead Bay, Brooklyn, where he first arranged for strings. He was there for eighteen months, playing at concerts, dances, and parades, having fun. Then he was abruptly declared 1-A; he reported for induction but was put into a bureaucratic limbo and told to wait. He then got the dream job: working in the Tommy Dorsey orchestra. Sinatra was gone, but Riddle was able to dig into the glorious library of Dorsey arrangements done by his friend Finegan, Eddie Sauter, and Hugo Winterhalter, along with earlier works by Sy Oliver and others. As a trombone player, Riddle admired Dorsey; he also liked him, which was not as easy.

"Tommy was pleasant to me in his own particular gruff way and quite supportive of my budding career as an arranger," Riddle said. "He was, and always will be, one of my heroes."

In April 1945 the army finally demanded the immediate services of Nelson Riddle. The war was almost over, and Riddle never left the United States. For "fifteen fun-packed months" he worked in an army band, and was discharged in June 1946. But during his army service, his teeth were knocked out in an accident; he was never able to play trombone effectively again and was forced to commit to arranging and, he hoped, composing. He freelanced around New York for a few months and then left for the West Coast, where he thought he had a job with

the Bob Crosby orchestra; that gig evaporated almost as
soon as he arrived, and he cobbled together a living as a
freelancer. Like millions of other young men, he also
took advantage of the educational benefits of the GI Bill,
which for Riddle meant studying with an Italian composer named Mario Castelnuovo-Tedesco. "His method of
teaching orchestration was to have his young pupils
study a piece written for piano and assign the voices, or
lines, in the piano solo to various sections or solo instruments of the orchestra. I found this process to be a most
instructive and broadening experience, since many of his
pianistic examples were works of such brilliant and di-
versified composers as Albéniz, Schubert, Brahms, Debussy and many more."

Riddle always credited Castelnuovo-Tedesco with giving him "skill and fluency" in handling large groups of
instruments and later regretted that his commercial success forced him to cut short his studying after two years.
At the same time, Riddle was studying with a Russian
named Victor Bay, who taught him the rudiments of conducting. Through this period his family was growing; to
support his wife and three children, he arranged music
for NBC Radio and freelanced for film composer Victor
Young. He took whatever other work he could get, as
Sinatra would say later, to put food on the table; some
members of the Depression generation never had the
psychological luxury of turning down jobs. But in 1950
and 1951 he broke through. He had arranged, without

credit, two tunes for the singer and jazz pianist Nat Cole. One was "Mona Lisa." The other was "Too Young." Each was a gigantic hit. Cole insisted that he wanted Riddle for his future work, and Riddle soon joined the staff at Capitol Records. He was there when Frank Sinatra arrived in the spring of 1953.

The odd thing was that Sinatra didn't seem to know much about the thirty-one-year-old Riddle when they did their first session together on April 30, 1953. Perhaps he was too absorbed in the melodrama of the Fall to notice the huge success of "Mona Lisa" and "Too Young"; perhaps he just didn't want to know about it. But according to Will Friedwald, in his exhaustive (and excellent) book *Sinatra! The Song Is You*, Sinatra thought he was cutting four sides by bandleader-arranger Billy May. In fact, Riddle, with May's agreement, had arranged two tunes in May's style and two in his own. When Sinatra saw Riddle in the studio, his first question was "Who's he?"

Assured that Riddle was only conducting, because May was on the road with his own band, Sinatra recorded "South of the Border" and "I Love You." Both had some of the slurping saxophone mannerisms of Billy May, and Sinatra sounded better than he had in years. Then they turned their attention to "I've Got the World on a String," written in 1932 by Harold Arlen and Ted Koehler for a Cotton Club revue. Sinatra had sung it in clubs and a few larger venues, using an arrangement from an old radio show. But he had never done it this way. With its wonderful decrescendo opening and the passionate trombone playing of Milt Bernhart, the recording was their first masterpiece.

Years later, Alan Dell, then a Capitol executive, gave Friedwald an account of the session. When it was over, Sinatra said, "Hey, who wrote that?" Dell replied, "This guy, Nelson Riddle." Sinatra said, "Beautiful!" Dell added, "And from that the partnership started."

That partnership would include 318 recordings made over the next quarter of a century. Sinatra recorded with many other arrangers, including Billy May, but Riddle brought a special sound to the work that became the mature sound of Frank Sinatra, the sound of the Comeback, the sound of the years when Sinatra always wore a hat and truly seemed to have the world on a string. The relationship wasn't always easy; according to Riddle, Sinatra was one of those men incapable of paying compliments to the people he truly admired. He expressed approval with silence; if he thought something wasn't working, he said so. Each had taken from Tommy Dorsey a sense of discipline and excellence.

"Frank and I both have, I think, the same musical aim," Riddle said in 1961. "We know what we're *each* doing with a song, what we want the song to say. The way we'd work is this: he'd pick out all the songs for an album and then call me over to go through them. He'd have very definite ideas about the general treatment, particularly about the pace of the record and which areas should be soft or loud, happy or sad. He'd sketch out something brief, like, 'Start with a bass figure, build up second time through and then fade out at the end.' That's possibly all he would say. Sometimes he'd follow up with a phone call at three in the morning with some other extra little idea. But after that he wouldn't hear my arrangement until the recording session."

Sinatra also admired Riddle's care for details: "Nothing ever ruffles him. There's a great depth somehow to the music he creates. And he's got a sort of stenographer's brain. If I say to him at a planning meeting, 'Make the eighth bar sound like Brahms,' he'll make a cryptic little note on the side of some crappy music sheet and, sure enough, when we come to the session the eighth bar will be Brahms. If I say, 'Make like Puccini,' Nelson will make exactly the same little note and that eighth bar will be Puccini all right, and the roof will lift off."

There were a number of components to the Sinatra-Riddle collaboration. Friedwald emphasizes one of them: "Lightness shines as the primary ingredient of the Riddle style. Whether he has ten brass swinging heavily or an acre of strings, Riddle always manages to make everything sound light; that way, the weightiest ballad doesn't become oversentimental and insincere, and the fastest swinger doesn't come off as forced."

The many records Sinatra made with Gordon Jenkins don't have this quality; the strings are heavy, gloppy, like musical cream cheese, and Sinatra's own ironical readings often sound more sentimental than they really are, because they are overwhelmed by the heaviness of the arrangements. Riddle was always too hip to clog the music with a lot of sugar.

"A lot of musicians and writers don't get the full value out of a tune," Miles Davis said in 1958. "[Art] Tatum does and Frank Sinatra always does. Listen to the way Nelson Riddle writes for Sinatra, the way he gives him enough room and doesn't clutter it up. Can you imagine how it would sound if Mingus were writing for Sinatra? But I think Mingus will settle down; he can write good music. But about Riddle, his backgrounds are so right that sometimes you can't tell if they're conducted."

Riddle's own distinctive sound almost always included flutes; a muted, commenting trumpet played by Harry (Sweets) Edison, who provided accents and emphases; trombones, of course; and a solid rhythm section. But he experimented with the combinations, always hoping to keep the sound fresh, while serving the needs of Sinatra as a singer. On the *Only the Lonely* album, for example, he used for the first time a full woodwind section, made up of two flutes, two oboes, two clarinets, and two bassoons. He would use that combination again and again, sometimes playing into and against sheets of strings, all of them united by harmonies he had absorbed from listening to Ravel, Debussy, and other impressionist composers.

"I loved how Nelson used Ravel's approach to polytonality," said Quincy Jones, who has written arrangements for everyone from Count Basie and Ray Charles to Michael Jackson. "Nelson was smart because he put the electricity up above Frank. He put it way upstairs and gave Frank the room downstairs for his voice to shine, rather than building big, lush parts that were in the same register as his voice."

Sinatra, the musician, was always involved in the actual execution of the complete piece of music.

"Frank accentuated my awareness of dynamics by exhibiting his own sensitivity in that direction," Riddle would later write. "It is one thing to indicate by dynamic markings ... how you want to have the orchestra play your music. It is quite another to induce a group of blase, battle-scarred musicians to observe those markings and to play accordingly. I would try, by word or gesture, to get them to *play correctly*, but if after a couple of times through, the orchestra *still* had not effectively observed the dynamics, Frank would suddenly turn and draw from them the most exquisite shadings, using the most effective means yet discovered, sheer intimidation."

Within a year they would combine on "Young at Heart," and Sinatra would have his first single to make the top five since 1947. The amazing comeback would be complete.

IV. While Sinatra was practicing his art with renewed vitality, he was still struggling to make sense of his private
life. The relationship with Ava Gardner remained jagged
and self-destructive. They were together, fought, split,
reconciled: a familiar pattern of obsession. The squalid
little drama was in horrid counterpoint to the rise in his
fortunes in other areas. In August *From Here to Eternity*
was released, and Sinatra received rave reviews. The
movie also shifted the way he was viewed by large numbers of men. Many seemed to merge Sinatra with Maggio, and when the thin, brave character of the movie is
beaten to death by the character played by Ernest Borg-
nine, it was a kind of symbolic expiation. Sinatra had
shown an aspect of his character that many had never
witnessed before in a Sinatra movie or heard singing
from jukeboxes. Sinatra/Maggio had lost. But in death,
he had won.

Before the movie opened, Sinatra had been booked
into Bill Miller's Riviera, on the New Jersey side of the
George Washington Bridge. Only a year before, he had
played that room to many empty tables. Now, suddenly,
the place was packed, celebrities were using pull to get
in, the parking lot was jammed, and even the gangsters
had problems getting tables. Sinatra was exultant.

At the same time, in the fall of 1953, Ava Gardner decided to end the marriage. Her account of the decision in
her autobiography has a kind of hard-boiled poignancy:

"I don't think I ever sat down and made a conscious

decision about leaving Frank; as usual I simply acted on impulse and allowed events to sweep me along. But I remember exactly when I made the decision to seek a divorce. It was the day the phone rang and Frank was on the other end, announcing that he was in bed with another woman. And he made it plain that if he was going to be constantly accused of infidelity when he was innocent, there had to come a time when he'd decide he might as well be guilty. But for me, it was a chilling moment. I was deeply hurt. I knew then that we had reached a crossroads. Not because we had fallen out of love, but because our love had so battered and bruised us that we couldn't stand it anymore."

Sinatra went on to win the Academy Award for best supporting actor. His records began selling. He appeared before large crowds in New York, Miami, and Las Vegas. Offers arrived every day for television shows and movie roles. But it took him a long time to get over Ava Gardner. She had decided to live in Europe, and he followed her to London and Spain, sometimes begging for a reconciliation that never happened. Back at home, without hope, the wounds slowly healing, he transformed himself into the Sinatra who wore a hat. The swinger whose best friends were men. The man with a lot of women, which was, of course, like having no woman at all. The message was there in the music, the attitude, even the hat: he had come through a hard, dark time, and he wasn't ever going back to the darkness.

But some of the hardest times in life never completely end. The only time I ever met Ava Gardner was in 1974. A mutual friend took me to see her. She had been drinking and kept whacking a small dog with a rolled-up tabloid newspaper. She was staying at Frank Sinatra's apartment in the Waldorf-Astoria.

V. By the mid-1950s Sinatra was expressing the feelings and yearnings of men. And they were listening. Most Americans love stories of redemption, of course, but men identify more often with the tale of the return of the hero, the man who comes back wearing the scars of battle, harder and wiser than he was when he left. Looking at, or listening to, Sinatra, particularly after the release of the masterful album called *In the Wee Small Hours,* men changed their attitude about Frank Sinatra. They identified with the personal drama of the Fall, with the cliché of the hero led astray by the vixen and his eventual release from her wiles. Or they embraced another cliché: he had paid his dues. At last. Such men once believed that everything had been too easy for Frank Sinatra. But now he had paid for his good luck and his endless hubris in the ways they had paid: with anguish and suffering and loss.

Even some of the old soldiers forgave him. The Korean War had confused all notions of the nobility of serving your country; it was an undeclared "police action," without a Pearl Harbor, and deepened the cynicism of many men. The fighting was ended in 1953 by the new president, Dwight Eisenhower, who knew as a general that it was folly to fight a land war in Asia. The men seemed to say, Don't trust history, trust only the personal. And for many men, the personal involved a merging of reality and fiction. In war or peace, they all knew men like Maggio.

On the records, the voice was deeper, richer, with more timbre, the voice of a man. But it also had a newer attitude. In the ballads, most of them torch songs, he was protected now with the armor of the stoic. The songs from *In the Wee Small Hours* said that in spite of loss, abandonment, defeat, he – and you – could get through the night. You could still get hurt, but it was worth the risk because you knew that no defeat was permanent. There would be another day, a new woman, another chance to roll the dice. There was rue in some of the songs. There was regret. There was no self-pity.

"Ava taught him how to sing a torch song," said Nelson Riddle many years later. "She taught him the hard way."

Everything that flowed from the comeback – the Rat Pack, the swagger, the arrogance, the growing fortune, the courtiers – is, in the end, of little relevance. It has as much to do with Sinatra's art as Hemingway's big-game hunting had to do with his. For a while Sinatra appeared to be the only man in America who could not be hurt again. Not ever. Onstage he exuded power and confidence; even the shadow of the Mob helped his image because it added a dangerous glamour to the performance and a dark resonance to his art. He made some good movies after the comeback: *The Man with the Golden Arm, Pal Joey, Some Came Running, High Society,* and *The Manchurian Candidate.* He also made some appalling, self-indulgent junk. But he simply didn't take acting seriously enough to become a great actor. Too often he settled for the first, most superficial take, avoiding the effort that would force him to stretch his talent, acting as if he were double parked. Too often, in too many movies, he cheated the audience and cheated himself. He never cheated in the music.

In the end, his most durable expression lies in that music. While living his life, Sinatra had learned something about human pain and found a way, through his music, to turn that hard-won knowledge into a form of human consolation. As the country changed, and the music along with it, as rock and roll took over and the baby boomers sneered at the children of Prohibition and the Depression, he was often baffled about the world and his role in it. But he continued practicing his own consoling art until the words and music could no longer rise from him into the trembling air.

Before leaving the stage, Sinatra had come to realize that life was not one long string of triumphs. As he grew older, he sometimes even floundered in the music (he made an entire album of songs based on Rod McKuen's ninth-rate poetry). But even his slumps did not last long. He could always find his way home to the music that had lasted him a lifetime, and almost until the end, he was capable of surprise. To be sure, much of what he did in life was also predictable. Watching the disorder and chaos of the sixties, his politics changed. But then, he was not the only old New Dealer who moved to the right, where he embraced Richard Nixon, a man he detested, and Ronald Reagan, a man he enjoyed. During that period of disorder he married and divorced Mia Farrow, who was thirty years his junior, and came away baffled at himself. "I still don't know what *that* was all about," he said to me a dozen years after it had ended. With his fourth wife, Barbara Marx, he retreated deeper into the bright, ritualized fortress he had erected in the California desert, far from the places that had hurt him into art. And I remember now a night I spent with him in 1974, driving around New York in a limousine, just talking.

"It's sure changed, this town," he said. "When I first came across that river, this was the greatest city in the whole goddamned world. It was like a big, beautiful lady. It's like a busted-down hooker now."

"Ah, well," I said. "Babe Ruth doesn't play for the Yankees anymore."

"And the Paramount's an office building," he said. "Stop. I'm gonna cry."

He laughed and settled back. We were crossing Eighty-sixth Street, heading for Central Park.

"You think some people are smart, and they turn out dumb," he said. "You think they're straight, they turn out crooked." This was the Watergate winter. The year before, Sinatra, the old Democrat, sat in an honored place at the second inauguration of Richard Nixon; the Watergate tapes would reveal a Nixon who retailed crude anti-Italian slurs. "You like people," Sinatra said softly, "and they die on you. I go to too many goddamned funerals these days. And women," he said, exhaling, and chuckling again. "I don't know what the hell to make of them. Do you?"

I said that every day I knew less.

"Maybe that's what it's all about," he said. "Maybe all that happens is, you get older and you know less."

I liked the man who talked that way on a chilly night in New York. I liked his doubt and his uncertainty. He had enriched my life with his music since I was a boy. He had confronted bigotry and changed the way many people thought about the children of immigrants. He had made many of us wiser about love and human loneliness. And he was still trying to understand what it was all about. His imperfections were upsetting. His cruelties were unforgivable. But Frank Sinatra was a genuine artist, and his work will endure as long as men and women can hear, and ponder, and feel. In the end, that's all that truly matters.

THE BACK OF
THIS BOOK

OVER THE YEARS I've learned much about Frank Sinatra and his music from a number of people, ranging from my old neighborhood friend, Bill Powers, to the great producer, Jerry Wexler. Nelson Riddle, while making his albums with Linda Ronstadt in the 1980s, also gave me insights into the man and his work. But across the years much of my instruction has come from Jonathan Schwartz. He is a fine writer, a musician, and a disc jockey at WQEW in New York. Sinatra once said of him: "He knows more about me than I do." Jonathan was generous in reading an early draft of this book and I am, again, in his debt. He is not, of course, responsible for errors that might have eluded both of us nor for my interpretations of the man and his music.

The Sinatra music has been scrambled and repackaged by various companies into a confusing mess. This was compounded by Sinatra himself, who for reasons of contractual argument, artistic dissatisfaction, or sheer laziness repeatedly went back to certain songs. But these albums are my own favorites: *In the Wee Small Hours, Songs for Swingin' Lovers, Only the Lonely, Come Fly with Me, A Swingin' Affair, Songs for Young Lovers, Come Dance with Me, Francis Albert Sinatra & Antonio Carlos Jobim, September of My Years, Sinatra at the Sands* (in spite of the wretched monologue), *Nice 'n' Easy,* and *Swing Along with Me.* There are a variety of boxed sets of his work at Columbia and earlier music with Tommy Dorsey and Harry James. All are rewarding, even the dumb novelties of the moment. I like the two-CD set from Columbia called *Portrait of Sinatra* and the five-CD package from RCA Victor called *The Song Is You,* which contains virtually all the Tommy Dorsey recordings. It is particularly interesting as a means of tracing the musical lessons learned by Sinatra from Dorsey. Needless to say, reactions to anyone's music are always subjective, but for me, the above albums offer many pleasures.

■ ■ ■

In writing this book, I was informed, entertained, or enriched in various ways by the following works:

Bacall, Lauren. *Lauren Bacall by Myself.* New York: Ballantine, 1978.

Behr, Edward. *Prohibition: Thirteen Years That Changed America.* New York: Arcade Publishing, 1996.

Carner, Gary. *The Miles Davis Companion.* New York: Schirmer, 1996.

Clarke, Donald. *All or Nothing at All.* New York: Fromm International, 1997.

Dellar, Fred. *Sinatra: His Life and Times.* New York: Omnibus Press, 1995.

Douglas-Home, Robin. *Sinatra.* New York: Grosset & Dunlap, 1962.

Ellis, Edward Robb. *A Nation in Torment: The Great American Depression, 1929-1939.* New York: Kodansha, 1995.

Farrow, Mia. *What Falls Away.* New York: Doubleday, 1997.

Friedwald, Will. *Sinatra! The Song Is You.* New York: DaCapo Press, 1997.

Gambino, Richard. *Vendetta.* New York: Doubleday, 1977.

Gambino, Richard. *Blood of My Blood.* Buffalo, N.Y.: Guernica, 1997.

Gardner, Ava. *Ava: My Story.* New York: Bantam, 1990.

Immerso, Michael. *Newark's First Ward.* New Brunswick, N.J.: Rutgers University Press, 1997.

Kelley, Kitty. *His Way.* New York: Bantam, 1986.

La Sorte, Michael. *La Merica.* Philadelphia: Temple University Press, 1985.

Lahr, John. *Sinatra: The Artist and the Man.* New York: Random House, 1997.

Lees, Gene. *Singers and the Song II.* New York: Oxford University Press, 1998.

O'Brien, Ed with Robert Wilson. *Sinatra 101.* New York: Boulevard Books, 1996.

Petkov, Steven and Leonard Mustazza. *The Frank Sinatra Reader.* New York: Oxford University Press, 1995.

Riddle, Nelson. *Arranged by Nelson Riddle.* New York: Warner, 1985.

Ringgold, Gene and Clifford McCarty. *The Films of Frank Sinatra.* Secaucus, N.J.: Citadel Press, 1993.

Sinatra, Nancy. *Frank Sinatra, My Father.* New York: Pocket Books, 1985.

Taraborrelli, J. Randy. *Sinatra: Behind the Legend.* Secaucus, N.J.: Carol Publishing, 1997.

Vare, Ethlie Ann, ed. *Legend: Frank Sinatra and the American Dream.* New York: Boulevard Books, 1995.

■ ■ ■

The Sinatra movies that remain worth seeing are:
Anchors Aweigh (1945),
On the Town (1949),
From Here to Eternity (1953),
Suddenly (1954),
Young at Heart (1955),
The Man with the Golden Arm (1955),
High Society (1956),
The Joker Is Wild (1957),
Pal Joey (1957),
Some Came Running (1958),
The Manchurian Candidate (1962),
and *The Detective* (1968).